D1046920

American Political Parties

Americar

Judson L. James

Political Parties

Potential and Performance

American Political Parties is part of a series, "Studies in Contemporary American Politics," published by Pegasus under the General Editorship of Richard E. Morgan, Columbia University.

Library of Congress Catalog Card Number: 79-77133

For Lawrence H. Chamberlain,
who exemplifies the true dignity of the phrase,
"a gentleman and a scholar."

preface

THIS BOOK attempts to unite two concerns, one empirical, the other normative. Their overlap and interdependence make the description and evaluation of American political parties a complex and necessary task, especially at a time when controversy about American political institutions is growing and political party reform generates widespread public debate.

The central focus in studies of American political parties has varied widely, including: party organization; voting behavior; parties in the governing process; and analysis of doctrines about party performance and function. Each type of study has given priority to different aspects of partisan activity, and they often have not been closely related to each other. Therefore, one of the principal aims of this book is to concentrate on continuities in partisanship and to present a unified empirical description of American political parties.

The evaluative concern arises out of the impact of political parties on the achievement of democratic government. The doctrinal analysis of democratic theory and political party functions therefore must be closely related to the empirical description of current party performance. To this end, five prototypes of possible normative and functional relationships are developed and compared to various aspects of partisan activity.

In the light of this two-fold analysis, the American party system appears to be more coherent, democratic, and responsible than it is often given credit for. This finding is especially important at a time when some of the most widely urged reforms would probably make parties less democratic and responsible, contrary to the reformer's intentions. It would be unfortunate if a combination of public impatience and ignorance permitted underevaluation of the accomplishments and potential of political parties in the United States. There are useful avenues of reform toward a more democratic and responsible party system which this volume explores; but to be effective, such reform requires an adequate assessment of the strengths of the present system as well as its weaknesses.

Because social and economic inequalities have prevented political equality, the United States has achieved only a limited degree of democratic government, due substantially to the development and activity of political parties. Although their internal structure and organization have not been thoroughly democratic, in their consequences for the society, American political parties are the institutions which have most effectively contributed to the goal of democratic government.

While I am willing to accept responsibility for all the factual and interpretative errors (there being no competing claimants), a number of people deserve credit for any virtues this book may have:

My teachers at Columbia University, whose encouragement and guidance led me to the concerns that dominate this book and helped to give me the skills the task required,

The late V. O. Key, Jr., of Harvard University, to whom every student of American political parties is deeply indebted,

Denis G. Sullivan, of Dartmouth College, for many conversations which developed and sharpened the major concepts and perspectives of this work in its early stages,

Gerald M. Pomper, of Rutgers University, whose thorough

and perceptive critique of earlier drafts corrected many errors and greatly improved the presentation of ideas. I also profited from his work on American elections, in addition to the time he generously took from it to assist me with his comments,

Gordon J. Schochet, of Rutgers University, who labored valiantly to educate me about the problems of democratic theory,

My students at Rutgers University and City College, whose demands for better explanations greatly enhanced the clarity of this presentation,

The American Political Science Review; The Johns Hopkins University Press; John Wiley and Sons, Inc.; and the Michigan Survey Research Center for their generous permission to reprint tables used in this book.

Richard E. Morgan, of Columbia University, whose editorial advice and encouragement moved my ideas into manuscript, and

Dorothy James, of Lehman College, City University of New York, who typed too many drafts to bear mentioning and corrected my prose toward readability. Her encouragement, among her many other wifely and scholarly virtues, enabled this work to be completed.

Judson L. James
January 1969

contents

list of tables

I. democratic theory and political parties

FOR VARIED and often contradictory reasons, many Americans are unhappy with their political parties. This dissatisfaction is part of a broader disagreement over the best means to achieve democratic government. Traditionally, democratization of political institutions has been the most important service provided by political parties and a widespread popular failure to appreciate this function poses a considerable threat to the maintenance of democracy. Consequently, a broader understanding of the intimate connection between democratic government and the political parties is vital to the American public.

An adequate discussion of the political parties in the United States should begin with a review of democratic theory and the nature of democratic government. There is a significant omission in the former—an absence of specific discussion on the way in which majority rule and popular consultation should actually be established and maintained. Political parties have developed as a response to this problem. Because democratic theory made this crucial omission, rival models or prototypes of the appropriate organization and purpose for political parties have developed. An analysis of the five principal prototypes which developed in the United States illustrates these differences and their consequences for American politics.

Defining Democracy

Great care is required in defining democracy.[1] Because it is generally a term of approval, it has been broadly used to describe any practices that people favor and wish others to regard as good, such as people's democracy, guided democracy, or democratic capitalism.[2] It is particularly necessary to distinguish between democracy as a way of life and democracy as a form of government—two radically different concepts—and then to define more specifically the concept more relevant to contemporary American politics.

Democracy as a way of life requires social and/or economic equality and therefore has an egalitarian emphasis beyond the political sphere. The quality of policy output, the fairness and justice it produces from an egalitarian social viewpoint, is the standard of judgment. Under this definition, modern regimes with at least nominally egalitarian social policy claim the title of democracy, although their governmental forms and procedures are totalitarian in nature.

As a form of government, democracy neither assumes nor requires social or economic equality, although it may provide opportunity for egalitarian tendencies. Instead, it prescribes a series of necessary political procedures. The crucial factor is *how* governmental policy is made, not *what* it is. "Democracy" in this sense is the more traditional definition, and the one on which the present analysis is based.

There are costs in defining democracy as a form of government rather than as a way of life; some important issues and problems in democratic theory are slighted. For example, democratic procedures, especially majority rule, could lead to "intolerable" policies by "democratic" criteria. Limited majority rule is a device designed to deal with this problem, but it may not be an adequate solution either, because a homogeneous and established majority could control all the significant veto points designed to protect minorities, for example, a white community unsympathetic to the grievances of a black minority in the United States.[3] Since democracy can potentially produce "unfair" results, it is desirable to demonstrate that it may also be the best way to ward off such possibilities and remedy them if they do occur.

Four principles are persistent and basic enough in the writing of most democratic theorists to justify describing them as a basic consensus on the nature of democracy and as requisite to democratic government. These are popular sovereignty, political equality, popular consultation, and majority rule.[4] Each principle is directly related to the characteristics and performance of political parties.

Popular sovereignty means that the people as a whole is the final source of governmental authority and legitimacy. It is the final court of appeal and can even dissolve the government and begin anew. This does not mean that the population as a whole acts directly to determine policy, but that it has the right to judge those who do. This right is superior to that of any official, group of officials, institution, or other group in the political community. Thus democratic government is "of the people" in the sense that it is derived from and based on the people's will.

Political parties can facilitate popular sovereignty by providing one possible mechanism by which the people can be mobilized. Without such a mechanism, the legitimacy of the final appeal to the people could not be made effective in operation. If popular opposition were diffuse and uncoordinated, leaders would be immune to challenge.

Political equality is the unrestricted opportunity to participate in the political process. It is more than "one man, one vote," because voting is not the only means of influencing decisions and is not complete in itself. The recent use of a plebiscite to ratify a new constitution in Greece, for example, demonstrates the compatibility of "one man, one vote" with contemporary totalitarianism. A voting choice is not enough unless there are real alternatives, public knowledge about the consequences of these alternatives, and freedom to choose without reprisals. Participation prior to the vote enables the citizen to shape the alternatives presented, to inform himself on the choices, and to affect decisions remote from or unsuitable as the focus of an electoral campaign.

The fact that political parties can broaden the bases of popular participation fosters political equality. It is therefore in their interest to involve previously uncommitted groups in politics. To gain and retain this support, the parties must be responsive to the concerns of these recruited supporters. Furthermore, the wide scope of partisan activity links a variety of policymaking centers, both legislatures and administrative bodies, to the choices made in elections. Party competition promotes the voicing of partisan alternatives and limits the authority of the governing party, which adds meaning to the electoral choice. The chapters below on voting behavior, party government, and competition develop these themes further.

Popular consultation requires that the popular will be made known to officeholders and that they in turn execute it as public policy; so democratic government must remain always responsive to the wishes of the people on matters of public policy. Not only must the popular will be accurately known, but the transmission of popular attitudes to the office holders must also be reinforced by a popular capacity to penalize officials who are not responsive, so that responsibility can be established and enforced. Of course, there may be no popular will or majority opinion on a given subject, and officials need not be greatly limited by diffuse attitudes or indifference.

Popular consultation is heavily dependent on political parties and interest groups. Political parties are motivated to discover popular preferences as a means to electoral success. The party which is out of power can punish the incumbents by appealing to popular preferences that incumbents have neglected; and by finding common ground in diffuse, conflicting minority views, it can create popular majorities for its own candidates.

Majority rule is both the most obvious and most controversial principle of democratic government. Limits on majority rule are considered necessary to protect certain minority rights, especially those crucial to effective political participation, but these limits must usually be enforced by formal vetoes or requirements for extraordinary majorities for governmental action on particular issues. As a result, the means of protecting minority rights can sometimes create minority rule, thus negating popular consultation and political equality on certain issues. Moreover, the tyranny possible in absolute majority rule on all matters is usually overstated. Although the majority is the ultimate source of authority, minorities may prevail on specific issues as long as the majority is not intensely opposed to the outcome. Normally "minorities rule,"[5] and it is important to remember that the justification for majority rule is not its monopoly on correct decisions, but its function in maintaining political equality. If a minority can continually prevail, its members are more equal and freer to choose than the members of the majority.

In practice, the difference between absolute majority rule and limited majority rule of democratic governments is less than these abstract alternatives imply. Governments with absolute majority rule have to defer occasionally to intense minorities to maintain political stability. Formal vetoes on majority preferences are not always exercised if the preference is intense. Prudent democratic government requires restraint by both the advantaged majorities and the advantaged minorities.

The party role in achieving popular consultation is closely related to its functions in enhancing majority rule. Political parties require popular majorities for political success; it is therefore in the selfish interest of party leaders to create popular majorities by whatever means are available. This is especially significant in creating and organizing alternatives in general elections.

Crucial Omission

The attempt to apply principles of popular sovereignty, political equality, popular consultation, and majority rule to contemporary government reveals problems inherent in the early formulations of democratic theory. These problems focus on the role of intermediate institutions connecting the people to their government and raise questions particularly about the means of achieving satisfactory popular consultation and majority rule, the principles on which political parties have their greatest impact. Political equality depends much more on the way in which political resources are distributed by the social and economic order than on political parties.

The application of these four democratic principles is clearest in the simplest form of democratic government, the New England town meeting (or the seemingly similar Greek city-state). In the periodic town meeting, political equality and popular sovereignty are achieved by the participation of any and all in both the discussion and choice of policy. Popular consultation is inherent in the ease with which the popular will can be expressed and implemented by the town meeting's collective decisions. Finally, majority rule is the criterion of decision.

But the simplicity and clarity of democratic government achieved in the town meeting is not easily duplicated in a nation of modern dimensions and complexity.[6] Popular sovereignty cannot be exercised directly because the population cannot be assembled in one place and time. Therefore, representative processes and a system of delegating government authority must be created. Political equality is threatened by the resulting inequalities of participation in and information about the formation of public policy. New ways of conveying the popular will to the officeholders and ensuring that they will obey it must be found. How will dispersed majorities be organized and recognized? What is needed to ensure that the majorities will in fact prevail in the decisions made? These sorts of problems led many democratic theorists (especially Rousseau) to despair of achieving democratic government beyond the physically compact boundaries of the city-state or the comparably small New England town.

The main issue is the application of the abstract principles central to democratic theory to the government of large, industrialized nations. To conclude that this is impossible both overrates the actual practice of the town meeting and understates the democratic potential of the nation-state.[7] The problem is how to organize and structure the relation of the people to its agent, the government. Classical democratic theorists did not pay a great deal of attention to the problem of staffing and operating the institutions of government they prescribed. They virtually ignored politics, which is the process whereby government policies are developed, decided, and enforced. After describing the necessary distribution of governmental powers and electoral rules, the steps to actual government policy were only superficially suggested. Politics was assumed to be automatic; but in actual practice, of course, means had to be developed to relate people to their government. John Locke, for example, prescribed the property qualifications for voting members of Parliament but said nothing about the appropriate internal direction and organization of the governing body itself.[8]

This gap between theory and practice was not merely a historical issue. It led many of the most influential democratic theorists to ignore or denounce precisely those rudimentary developments which were in time to provide the necessary link between the sovereign (the people) and its agent (the government, that is, the intermediate political institutions. The many narrowly based factions of personality, family, region, and commercial interest which were the principal active agents in the early representative assemblies were especially repugnant to early writers on democracy. Rousseau defined faction as necessarily narrow and selfish and asserted that representative assemblies had their own special interest, contrary to the General Will of the people. Therefore, he maintained, all representative mechanisms are corrosive of democracy.[9] Other theorists were more hopeful of representative assemblies, but denounced "factional" politics as it occurred in the late eighteenth- and nineteenth-century parliaments and congresses.

This distaste for factions was particularly important in the development of political theory because factionalism was the initial stage in the growth of more specialized institutions—political parties and interest groups. Through factions and their successors, some basic requirements of democratic government could be achieved.[10] Political leaders, representatives, and rulers were selected, and participation in that choice widened. Rulers and governments could be changed, all within the context of a stable regime. Elements of public opinion were represented and connected to the formation of public policy. Various aspects of governmental authority were organized, controlled, and connected.

Since factionalism was considered illegitimate in classical

democratic theory, its descendants have never been accorded full legitimacy in democratic political thought.[11] Classical theorists ignored the need for a link between government and people, and politics became a pejorative word whose institutions were suspect. Consequently, the role of political parties in achieving democratic government was obscured.

Party Prototypes

From this ambiguity in democratic theory, rival interpretations developed as to the appropriate way of organizing political parties best to serve democratic government. The alternatives have been regarded since as the prototypes or models of what political parties should be. In the United States, a preference for limited government and the resulting need to coordinate dispersed authority has generated five basic prototypes.

The American interpretation of democratic theory, expressed in the dominant characteristics of American government, deemphasizes majority rule to protect minority rights. Americans emphasize and glory in decentralization and checks and balances. The federal system, the separation of executive and legislature, written constitutions, and judicial review all reflect the desire to ensure individual freedom by limiting government. These limitations operate by setting parts of the government against other parts. Diffusion of authority creates a great number of centers of power, each with considerable capacity to veto the initiatives and programs of others. Negative government is therefore explicit in the design and impact of the governmental structure; the American government is deliberately decentralized and limited.

It is important to stress the implications of the governmental structure for those issues and occasions when government activity might be necessary or desirable. Any initiative or innovation of policy requires coordinating these centers of power. For example, a legislative act must survive the decisions of two Houses, several committees, the executive, the courts, and administrative follow-through. The greater the scope and impact of the innovation, the greater the number and variety of diffused centers of government authority that will have to be coordinated to give full effect to the innovation.

Therefore, the relation of political parties to the structure of government is twofold. Because governmental authority is widely distributed, competition for this authority creates multiple centers of influence within the party. But parties also provide informal coordination of the dispersed formal government structure. The presence of partisans throughout the structure makes continuity in government action possible. Thus parties are advantageously placed to assume responsibility for governing.

The limitations on majority rule and the coordination potential of political parties point to two principal classifying dimensions for the five party prototypes—one normative, the other empirical. The normative dimension is the degree of preference for majority rule. A preference for positive innovative government is usually associated with a strong majority rule position; a concern for protecting minorities is more compatible with negative government and a status-quo policy preference. The empirical dimension is one's estimate of the capacity of political parties to coordinate successfully the diffuse, decentralized government structure. Closely associated with this is the question of how to effect adequate popular consultation. Proponents of each of the five prototypes are engaged in a quarrel therefore both about the *capacity* of American political parties and the *desirability* of unlimited majority rule. It is this conjunction of normative and factual questions that makes the debate about American political parties so complex.

Evidence that these dimensions (majority rule and capacity to coordinate) are essential to each prototype may be found in the fact that they can be used to relate each to the other. In the table on page 24, the two dimensions are used to define the possible alternatives, ranging from absolute majority rule to minority protection and from great capacity to coordinate government to none. In principle, a party prototype could combine these dimensions in a wide variety of ways. For purposes of clarity and because these terms are already coined and in use, five descriptions cover the basic alternatives. They represent adequately the range of choices in discussions on party structure and the objectives that are represented in scholarly writings, popular attitudes, regulatory legislation, the beliefs of political leaders, and the actual operations of American political parties. They are: Party Government, Responsible Parties, Progressive, Nonpartisan, and Status Quo. (The distinction here between Party Government and Responsible Parties prototypes imposes a clarity that is usually lacking as these terms are customarily used. However, this definition does reflect the differences, in degree at least,

TABLE I

MAJOR PROTOTYPES OF PARTY PURPOSES AS VIEWED BY THEIR PROPONENTS

Preference of Proponents Concerning Majority Rule	Estimate by Proponents of the Capacity of Political Parties to Coordinate Government		
	Great Capacity for Coordination	Some Capacity for Coordination	No Capacity for Coordination
Absolute majority rule	**Party Government**		**Progressive**
Qualified majority rule		**Responsible Parties**	
Oppose majority rule	**Nonpartisan**		**Status Quo**

among the many analysts who have urged more responsible parties and/or party government.)

Party Government proponents believe that political parties can coordinate the government and wish to use them to enhance majority rule. Nonpartisans concede the capabilities of political parties but oppose them because they are opposed to majority rule. Progressives believe that strong party organizations are a barrier to majority rule, which they wish to accomplish despite the parties. Proponents of the Status Quo argue that political parties cannot coordinate government and that this is no great loss since they oppose absolute majority rule. The Responsible Parties proponents acknowledge the limits on party coordination created by the complexities of American government and settle for less than absolute majority rule. Their position is intermediate on the two classifying dimensions, and stands midway between the other four prototypes.

Since coordination of the diffuse, decentralized government structure enhances the possibility for positive, innovative government, a preference for such innovation is closely related to one's attitude on majority rule. The party prototypes reflect this parallel. The Nonpartisan position is held by those who believe that parties can coordinate and innovate in government policy but who do not want innovation. The Status Quo advocate decries both the need and the possibility of party coordination of government. Party Government supporters want extensive policy changes and feel that the political party is the best mechanism for accomplishing them. Progressives want policy change also, but doubt the usefulness of political parties. The Responsible Parties advocates again take an intermediate view. They want moderate policy changes and are concerned about both the limits on, and the possibilities of, government policy coordination by means of political parties.

Each prototype will be discussed individually below. For each, the motivations, mechanisms, probable consequence, and possible criticisms and costs will be examined, along with their implications for popular consultation and majority rule.

Party Government

Party Government is desired by those who wish to ensure majority rule, effective and rapid decisions, and clear responsibility for government action by the incumbent party. Its advocates stress a need for the following attributes in American political parties: party discipline, party programs, elections as mandates, and centralized party leadership.[12] The emphasis on party discipline is central to their conception. They desire a comprehensive party program so that they can define the party clearly and differentiate it from its competitors. Voter choice between two contrasting major parties would, in their view, render elections a mandate for the program of the winning party. Central leadership of this party would support internal discipline and fulfillment of the party program.

Advocates of Party Government feel a very urgent need for government action. They believe that foreign threats and domestic problems require drastic, broad programs as remedies. Because the delay and variety of responses permitted by a diffuse government structure can defeat rapid and consistent action, they desire coordination of the entire governmental system.

Party Government support is closely related to support of ideological parties. The party program need not be ideologically based, but that is a very likely outcome. Moreover, the emphasis on the need for broad and rapid innovation parallels the impatient outlook of ideologues, both right and left. It is not surprising, therefore, that right-wing Republicans and left-wing Democrats share enthusiasm for two more homogeneous parties with drastically different and ideologically based programs.

Among the costs of establishing Party Government in the United States would be virtual elimination of the federal system and of separated branches of the government structure. These changes would be a necessary step in building a Party Government system (something its advocates often do not clearly recognize or acknowledge) because federalism and separated branches of government create incentives for internal party conflict, and so reduce the possibilities for coordination. A single focus is necessary if a party is to achieve an authoritative program and the centralized leadership that alone can maintain disciplined adherence to that program.

Another possible cost of Party Government might be a multi-party system. It is not clear that all the major policy options could be gathered under two major programs and parties. Multi-partyism could lead in turn to ineffective government and failure of majority rule, negating the central virtues of the Party Government proposal. In addition, programmatic parties might sharpen ideological conflict and emphasize the social, economic, and political divisions between the supporters of the various parties. Majority decisions might become more drastic, cumulative, and unacceptable to the minority. The willingness to support the outcomes of elections and of government decisions could decrease, reducing the long-run stability and community support necessary for the political process.

To these hypothetical problems, advocates of Party Government reply that any majority in a highly pluralistic culture would have to be moderate. In order to assemble its majority in the first place from diverse groups, it would have to minimize points of conflict by finding a lowest common denominator for them. This approach parallels Madison's argument in *The Federalist: 10* that a large republic is less likely to contain a tyrannical majority than a relatively homogeneous smaller community. At the same time, it directly contradicts the criticism that Party Government is impossible because programmatic parties will create multi-party systems. Critics cannot be allowed to have it both ways: the society cannot be both too pluralistic to allow only two parties and so easily and sharply divided into two camps that civil war may threaten.

With a solid base on majority rule and electoral mandate, the cohesion and discipline of the incumbent party is expected to provide effective, positive government. The Party Government prototype focuses on the functioning of the governing party and the efficient rendering of majority will into government policy. Popular consultation is here regarded as a very simple and direct process.

In return for these benefits, Party Government makes major demands on the American political process. It requires that each national party exercise significant control over local nominations, especially for Congress, otherwise party discipline could not be maintained or the party program uniformly supported. The party leadership needs to control the influence and opportunities of national executive and legislative officials. The seniority system and/or permanent committees of Congress would have to be put to an end, in order to eliminate independent centers of power. To reduce the impact of state and local political competition, voting decisions would have to be made solely in terms of responses to the national party programs. The voters must be mobilized and respond on this basis if elections are going to provide a clear-cut mandate for a particular program.

The Party Government prototype poses two major questions. First, can such drastic reforms in the structure of the government and the parties be justified? Decentralized nominations, the separation of branches of government, and the federal structure all represent major choices that deliberately reduce the likelihood of positive, innovative government. The severity of this conflict with established values presents a considerable problem in persuasion. Second, are voters likely to behave as they must to make Party Government work? Party programs organized around national issues must involve and control the choice of the entire electorate if the mandate of the majority party is to be beyond question. The relevance here of studies of voting behavior will be explored in Chapter IV.

The sweeping nature of the reforms required by the Party Government prototype has led many to doubt both its possibility and desirability. A more modest program is that for responsible parties.

Responsible Parties

The Responsible Parties prototype differs more in degree than kind from Party Government. In fact, many discussions use the terms almost interchangeably, which creates confusion so far as this analysis is concerned. Nevertheless, the differences in degree are sufficient to merit separate consideration, because they are consistent enough to create a distinctive outlook on the requirements for party and for government.[13] Both majority rule and popular consultation are considered generally more complex by the advocates of Responsible Parties.

Supporters of this position are modest in their aspirations; while concerned with change, they are less impatient than the Party Government advocates. Political parties are viewed as necessary to coordinate government and make innovation possible, but Party Government proper is regarded as neither possible nor desirable. They would agree with the critique of the Party Government prototype, especially in finding the necessary reforms far too drastic.

Party Government focused on achieving popular consultation by improving the performance in office of the governing party. Responsible Party advocates stress the relation of the party to the electorate, and especially the extent to which the public can control the party; they emphasize the degree to which it is responsible to the electorate. For this reason, the opposition party is given relatively more attention, because it has a crucial responsibility in rendering *both* parties responsible. Much more than with Party Government, a two-party system is assumed.

Responsibility, as V. O. Key has suggested, does not necessarily require two *different* sets of potential rulers, merely two sets.[14] The threat that the opposition party might reap the fruit of popular dissatisfaction with the incumbents forces a concern for the popular will. The party out of power can often profit without an alternative program. In the Responsible Parties view, reliance is placed on the consequences of party competition rather than on the context of that competition. The self-interest of party leaders in party victory, it is claimed, leads them to a responsiveness to popular concerns and a pragmatic, piecemeal adoption of party programs. Parties could, of course, develop as moderately left and right of center alternatives as a response to vague pressures for innovation and consolidation, respectively.

The focus on responsibility rather than on actual program

is influenced by the limited means of expression available to the voter. Voting is a crude device for popular control. Regardless of how many candidates are running, the voter is limited in effect to saying Yes to one and No to the rest. Typically, ranking or distribution of support is impossible. When the voter is faced by an individual running for office, he cannot vote Yes on some of the candidate's policies and No on others. He must make a summary judgment, lumping the pros and cons as he may.

In trying to make this summary judgment, the voter is primarily concerned with the acts of the incumbent, whose past performance is better known and the usual focus of decision. But the attempt to hold individual officials responsible for the passage or failure of desired policies proves extremely difficult. The complexity of the dispersed government structure permits a great deal of buck-passing, obscurity, and ignorance about the nature of current public policy. Bills are buried in committee, sabotaged in their administration, and wittingly passed in a form that will lead to their veto elsewhere. The art of avoiding responsibility is a highly developed and effective one within a government structure which gives so many the capacity to defeat or modify measures. Few citizens can trace this process through for even a single piece of legislation.

It is these difficulties in enforcing individual responsibility that lead Responsible Parties supporters to argue that the continuing nature of the party label is a better path to responsible government. The sharing of a partisan identification should create shared risks for officeholders scattered throughout the government structure. A scandal or unpopular legislation while Republicans are in office, for example, will create a reaction against the Republicans generally, creating a hazard for personal careers. Thus, for their own self-protection, members of a party have an incentive to supervise fellow partisans who might create scandals or adopt unpopular policies.

By holding the incumbent party responsible for the acts of government, collective responsibility demands less of the voter, who has only to make the summary judgment on the incumbent administration. If his decision is No, he gives the opposition a chance to profit by the mistakes of the incumbent and a continuous motivation to expose the latter's errors. The Responsible Parties prototype favors actually giving up some capacity to enforce individual responsibility, in order to exert control over a wider range of officials by the principle of collective responsibility, as a superior means of achieving popular consultation.

The principal mechanisms of Responsible Parties rest on the possibility of shared involvement and risks under the party label. From this sharing should follow collective responsibility, simplification of electoral control by the general public, and party competition—without any need to specify the ideological or programmatic content of this competition.

Responsible Parties advocates differ most sharply from the Party Government prototype in their concern over having competitive parties at all levels of government. In the United States, political parties operate within national, state, and local government structures, all with major policy and administrative impact on the public. The states and localities vary quite widely among themselves in socioeconomic composition, past political history, and current government issues. Competing parties must therefore appeal to different voters on different grounds in one state or locality, as opposed to another. If a party was nationally uniform in its bases of support it might hold too large a share of the population in any given community to be stable or too small a share to generate effective competition. Its national programs might be largely irrelevant to the local issues, while in other communities its national appeals might doom it to an insignificant minority. If, for example, the New York and Arizona Republican parties were to be based on the same social groups and issues, one or both would be unable to compete effectively in their respective states. This follows from the very real differences between New York and Arizona in urbanization, ethnic distribution, economic bases, and political traditions.

It is the fact of competition within a number of heterogeneous constituencies that promotes the possibility of a heterogeneous party. The only means of making the parties uniform within the current American government structure is somehow to force them to compete solely for national offices, on uniform national issues and appeals. This is why the Party Government prototype must reduce the significance of federalism and local autonomy in nominations if it is to be feasible.[15] The Responsible Parties prototype, on the other hand, is assumed to be flexible enough to adjust to existing structures and retain their benefits. In each constituency the Republicans might be more conservative on average than the Democrats, although a conservative position would vary in content from constituency to constituency, depending on local issues and problems.

Responsible Parties doctrine consequently requires a more modest, although still extensive, set of reforms. The realignment of the Southern Democrats along the lines more generally prevailing in the rest of the nation would make the existing party system more rational and enhance competition at the state level; hopefully, there are general trends favoring realignment on the basis of socioeconomic status which will aid that situation. However, the basic point of Responsible Parties reform is to strengthen party organization, especially that of the minority party. The present weakness in the minority party's ability to compete handicaps the operation of collective responsibility. For reasons that will be developed more fully in Chapters II and III, the long ballot, legislative malapportionment, the direct primary, and related features of government structure, as well as the present nomination procedures, all gravely handicap the minority party.[16]

The Responsible Parties prototype attempts to link majority rule and popular consultation to diffused government authority by the modest and flexible device of collective responsibility. A compromise between the needs of positive government and the protections of limited government is the goal. The advocate of this position is prepared to tolerate the incomplete mobilization and coordination of the government structure that a heterogeneous party, the federal system, and separated branches of government entail. Popular consultation is expected to reflect this complexity. The goal is less ambitious and the desire for innovation less impatient than that of the Party Government supporters.

Status Quo

The guiding principle of the Status-Quo prototype is not majority rule but the theory of concurrent majorities.[17] Government structure should be dispersed so that every minority can safeguard its basic interests by exercising a veto on innovation at some point. The agent of majorities, the political party, should not be able to coordinate the government easily because that would reduce the significance of interest group vetoes.

Advocates of this position are relatively satisfied with the current party system, which they see as highly decentralized and irrational in basis of voter support, hence the label "Status Quo". They also are status quo in a second sense, the perceived need for government policy innovation. For them piecemeal, leisurely change is all that is necessary or desirable. That way, the basic interests of the minority are protected against the possibility of majority tyranny, because any successful major innovation would require every interested group's participation and accommodation. An unchecked majority rule, they believe, disregards the checks and balances needed to protect minorities. However, it should be noted here that the minorities this ideology protects most easily are status-quo minorities with established veto points in the government structure. For example, Southern whites have a greater use and need for veto power than blacks who require positive, innovative government action to remedy the consequences of past conditions. Understandably, therefore, most Southern whites prefer the status quo and negative government.

The looseness and structural weakness of existing parties is expected to provide open channels of recruitment for interested individuals, as well as opportunities for various social groups. These groups and individuals should advance their interests by rising through the party, accepting its procedures and compromises. In this way, the potentially disaffected are supposedly accommodated to the existing regime and social stability is enhanced. Protest would not be walled out and the ambitious would be rewarded within the defined structure and would therefore have few incentives to make careers outside it.

From the Status-Quo viewpoint, parties are also expected to provide stability by maintaining continuity in partisan affiliations. Such partisan attachments sometimes persist beyond the issues which generated them, so resulting in an irrational allegiance to parties whose programs are in fact contrary to current policy attitudes. Simple partisanship of this type is desirable from the Status-Quo viewpoint because it would moderate, confound, and decentralize political conflict. Thus partisan allegiances actually reinforce consensus by building support for party policy beyond the policy's immediate adherents.[18]

Political parties would provide only loose majority control over those who actually established policy. Both major parties would assemble heterogeneous majorities which would result in moderate policy. Since the parties would be similar to each other, a cross section of either would include virtually all population elements and could not oppress any minority without also oppressing some of its own supporters.

An advocate of the Status-Quo prototype has the simplest of tasks in defending his doctrine. He need only resist any measures or activities which would rationalize the basis of support or strengthen the organization of the political parties. Above all, he wants to damp the fires of political conflict and to use parties as broad coalitions in order to smooth the rough edges of ideological and programmatic factions. Parties are potentially disruptive if they divide on fundamental issues; but if weak in structure and confused in orientation, they are benign. They should be a channel for moderating the impact of popular participation, not enhancing it. Popular consultation and majority rule are therefore downgraded in favor of stability and the protection of established minorities.

Progressives

The Progressive prototype attempts to achieve direct democracy—majority rule and popular consultation operating, without intermediate institutions, from the people to the government. As a consequence of its origins, the Progressive prototype specifically rejects party organization as a mechanism for democratic government.

At the close of the nineteenth century, a reaction set in against the strong party organizations of the period. Under the banner of the Progressives, this reaction centered on the party leadership (or "bosses"). The existing party organization seemed to be a prime obstacle to the economic and political reforms which the Progressives wanted. They were therefore led to focus on the negative, rather than the positive aspects of party organization, and the reforms instituted as a result reflected the Progressive prototype of political parties.[19]

The Progressive impulse gives a low rating to intermediate political institutions: political parties, interest groups, even legislatures. It relies instead on an enlightened citizenry and the force of public opinion and prefers enforcing responsibility on the individual officeholder. Its supporters visualize the electorate as the aroused, well-educated sector of the middle class that formed much of the leadership and supplied the active workers in the Progressive movement.

Thus the major mechanisms and reform proposals of the Progressives are designed to achieve direct democracy by weakening party organization: nomination by direct and open primaries, referendum and initiative, civil service reform, recall, and internal democracy in party organization. Their fundamental attitude abhors party organization and favors reducing the barriers to wide citizen participation. Their reforms involve extensive regulation and specification of party organization. Party procedures and structure become the province of public law rather than the preserve of private voluntary associations.

Reform and innovation in government policy are also desired by the Progressives but, unlike the Party Government advocates, their immediate experiences lead them to believe that parties are a barrier to innovation. They place their confidence in the ability of the citizens to legislate directly (by means of referendum and initiative) and to nominate officials in an unstructured party (direct primary). Party organization is thought to have inherently evil tendencies, which require the curb of elaborate election laws. Civil service reform is instituted to reduce the incentive to participate in party organization. A reactionary strain in Progressive thought even seeks to restore the political purity of those seemingly more direct citizen-government relationships that were possible in a smaller and less complex nation in an earlier age.

Based on classical democratic theory and potent American political traditions, the Progressive model has been quite persuasive in twentieth-century America, especially in its impact on the organization of political parties today. The significance and impact of Progressive reforms calls for extensive analysis; this topic will be more fully developed in the discussion of party organization and nomination practices and developments in Chapter III.

The Progressive prototype therefore demands widespread, informed citizen participation; it sees party organization as largely devoid of any redeeming virtues; and it is quite optimistic about achieving a close approximation to direct democracy through its reforms.

Nonpartisan

The Nonpartisan position is opposed to majority rule, preferring instead a consensus solution that avoids the conflict normal in politics. It also downgrades popular consultation, since it favors technical solutions to government policy problems. Nonpartisanship is anti-party because it is fundamentally anti-pluralist. The stress on consensus opposes the recognition and expression of diverse interests and is in effect anti-democratic.

The Nonpartisan prototype rests on a distaste for politics itself, that is, for the conflict and the resolution of conflict over public policy. Politics is seen as a dirty business of compromise and the satisfaction of particular interests at the expense of the "public interest." The Nonpartisan is distressed by the conflict between values and interests that makes bargaining the predominant mode of the political process. There "ought to be" a consensus on such values and goals and it is "unpatriotic" to differ with the incumbent administration. Party strife appears to reduce the unity of the political community, the necessary consensus. In any case, the alternative of party conflict is considered artificial because it creates conflict where none need exist.[20]

Supporters of the Nonpartisan prototype, like supporters of the Status Quo, do not want innovation. But, unlike the Status Quo-adherents, Nonpartisans believe that political parties could successfully coordinate the government structure and so they want to destroy them, root and branch.[21] The Nonpartisan wants to abolish not only party organization, but also the party label. This is where he differs from the Progressive, who is antagonistic to party organization but believes he can achieve policy innovation by more direct democracy. The more conservative Progressives would, of course, be quite close to the Nonpartisans. Nonpartisans recognize the impact of party labels in organizing electoral behavior and have attempted to limit parties by the institution of the Nonpartisan ballot. Party organization activity is not only forbidden, it is to be denied any reward by disallowing party identification on the ballots. The voter is not given any cues toward partisan choices.

The Nonpartisan prototype takes an even more exalted view of the capacity of the electorate than does the Progressive. The voter is expected to know and directly assess each candidate, without any labels. Independence from party is thus promoted as a virtue. This flatters the self-identified independent and builds up the influence of the mass media, especially newspapers. The newspapers replace parties by giving cues to the voters, identifying and describing the candidates, enhancing the chances of those favored in coverage, and probably increasing the sensitivity of candidates to the policy line of the papers. (It is not surprising that many newspaper publishers are supporters of Nonpartisan elections.)

The strongest argument for Nonpartisan government is made at the local level, where the unity of interest of the political community can be most persuasively asserted. It is frequently stated that "There is no Democratic or Republican way to pave a street." With a consensus on values and interests, government is merely the technical application of these values in specific administrative situations. Therefore, elections should not be tests of strength between rival political and social groups but the means of selecting the best men, independent of misleading labels. Innovation in government policy has little relevance to the static situation presumed by a consensus on values and interests.

In local elections this ideal has considerable acceptance, but is it really tenable? There may, in fact, be a Democratic or Republican way to pave a street. Which residential areas, middle-income or working-class, will be done first? Will the paving favor the downtown business districts or access to the factories? What kinds of taxes or methods of payment will be used to finance the paving program—pay-as-you-go, balanced budgets, or floating a bond issue? Different social groups and political attitudes would give contrasting answers to such questions and their answers are characteristically expressed through parties.

Nonpartisans tend to ignore or obscure the fact that majorities are not spontaneously active—they need to be organized. Yet political parties are the only institutions based on majorities and majority rule. Moreover, Nonpartisan ballots result in a substantially lower voter turnout, which provides an advantage for élite groups able to mobilize voters for their particular interests.[22] This advantage renders the process of popular consultation incomplete and biased. The view of government as a technical administration enhances the role of élites and experts at the expense of the popular will and does so deliberately, if not candidly. The Nonpartisan position is unsympathetic to both popular consultation and majority rule.

Summary

The five prototypes differ widely on the need for innovative, positive government and the capacity of political parties successfully to coordinate the complex, fragmented government of the United States. More important, these differences represent critical differences on the desirability and means of achieving majority rule and popular consultation. Each prototype has to some extent influenced the attitudes toward, and institutions of, American politics and political parties. Each make assertions about the extent of party organization needed; the ideological propensities of voters; their awareness and concern about issues; the extent of institutional reform necessary; the value of reforms already adopted; the party's role in the governing process; and its impact on the individual voter.

If we clarify and make explicit the values and issues implicit in judging political parties, a sharper appreciation of the characteristics of American political parties is possible. The next five chapters will move from the abstract conceptual and normative problems to the reality of the current practice of American political parties. The significance and relationship of these practices can then be compared to the varied expectations of possible party achievements. Thus the performance of American political parties can be evaluated and the reasons for their successes and failures illuminated.

Chapters II and III will deal with the expectations and limitations of party competition and organization. Chapters IV through VI will demonstrate the role of the partisan voter in structuring American political parties and politics. The two concluding chapters summarize and characterize political parties in the United States, their present and future prospects. Here the essay returns to its starting point and principal theme, the interdependence of democratic government and an effective political party system in the United States.

II. competition

IT IS COMPETITION which reconciles the selfish interests of party leaders and candidates with the achievement of democratic government based on popular sovereignty, political equality, popular consultation, and majority rule. Competition for support between political parties, for example, provides choices for the voter, and the parties' need for workers draws many into party activity, broadening the scope of political participation. This need to appeal for support further provides an incentive for developing alternative policies and opposition to the incumbent party. Thus competition gives elections significance as a method of democratic control of government because it is the means through which a peaceful turnover of government leadership can be organized. Popular consultation is enhanced by the party's desire to reflect popular preference in order to capture office. Because opposition parties provide an instrument through which public opinion can act, the incumbent parties must anticipate public opinion and take responsibility for government acts.

Competition is typically the principal dimension used in classifying political party systems. The presumed superiority of competition in the American two-party system ranks highest among its claims to public support. Nevertheless, close party competition is uncommon, both outside and within the United States. Political sectionalism and minor parties are related to this failure to achieve party balance. Perhaps the most critical manifestation of the limitations on effective two-party competition in the United States is to be found among recent third party movements in the South.

Political Party Systems

A political party does not stand in isolation: the presence and character of other parties constantly shape its activities and significance. It is therefore necessary to talk rather of political party systems—that is, the relationship and functions of all political parties within the political community. This interdependence helps to define what any given party in the system will or will not do.

Political party systems are normally classified by the extent of competition and the number of competitors. There are modified one-party, multi-party, coalition one-party, two-party, and even two-plus party systems.[1] Different ways of organizing competition have decisive effects on the significance of political parties.

The two-party system is widely regarded as especially effective in achieving democratic government. A two-party system has an advantage over multi-party systems in that it automatically produces majorities for the winning candidate. Multi-party systems can frustrate majority rule either by plurality victories or complex vote redistribution, proportional representation, or runoff schemes of election. Each of these rewards minorities and discourages, to some degree, emphasis on majority rule.

The multi-party system diffuses responsibility for governing. Majority dissatisfaction with incumbents may lead to the support of a number of opposition parties divided so that the incumbents can win with a plurality or less of the vote cast. Nevertheless, multi-party systems can reflect the distribution of public opinion more accurately than the diffuse majorities produced by a two-party system. While stable government is not impossible in a multi-party system, it does seem to require that one party approach an absolute majority of support—as in Scandinavia.

Yet even if a two-party system is desirable, that does not explain why the United States has only two major parties. For all its supposed virtues this system is found in very few countries, even those which have a considerable degree of democratic government. Although many of the more democratic countries approach two-party systems, in that two parties are much larger than the remaining parties (e.g., Great Britain, Canada, or West Germany), their third parties are far more significant than any permanent third parties in the United States.[2] This would seem to indicate that there must be special circumstances in the United States favoring the two-party system. Three types of explanation are generally offered, which can be codified as "initial dualism," "political institutions," and "fundamental consensus."[3]

The argument for initial dualism takes a number of forms, but its essential thesis is that the original political conflicts in the United States were two-sided and that inertia and tradition have carried this dualism forward into different issues and times. Either two rival economic interests (urban/agrarian) or simple division of the ins (Hamilton and Adams) against the outs (Jefferson and Madison) could provide the starting point. The traditional rhetoric supporting the two-party system, plus common expectations, could have led to its institutionalization and maintenance. These arguments make heavy use of the so-called First Law of Social Behavior, which matches the First Law of Physical Mechanics—the prevalence of inertia.

Yet, every active politician tries to limit or eliminate competition if he can. Patronage or tacit agreements may serve to limit the efforts of the minority party.[4] Moreover, initial dualism gives a weak explanation of the persistence of two parties. After all, the American two-party system collapsed twice, in the 1820's and in the 1850's, and was reconstructed each time.

A more impressive line of explanation can be found in institutional factors of American government. The two most important influences are the single-member district with plurality election and the presidency. The only exceptions to plurality election are the Illinois General Assembly, a few city councils which use proportional representation, and seven Southern Democratic state primaries which have runoff primaries. Plurality elections help to maintain a two-party system because the third, fourth, and fifth candidates in the race are merely damaging the chances of those to whom they are closest, and drawing similar support. For example, an incumbent could be rejected by 60 per cent of the electorate and still be elected if two or more candidates divided the opposition vote so that none of them received more than 35 per cent. For this reason, maximum political effectiveness requires the formation of coalitions before elections, not bargaining afterward. The lesser parties are handicapped in recruiting candidates, money, and workers, not only by their dim prospects but also by the argument that their effort is self-defeating, because it weakens similar candidates and relatively strengthens the candidates who are more antagonistic to their attitudes and interests. The second party has a "monopoly of the opposition" because of this strategic advantage.[5]

Proportional representation, the allocation of offices by the percentage of votes cast for the party ticket, or the requirement of an absolute majority for election both postpone coalition formation. Separate identity can have direct rewards under proportional representation (as in the French Fourth Republic) but its institution is impossible with single-member districts. The requirement of an absolute majority postpones forming two coalitions until the runoff election and encourages the maintenance of factional organization for bargaining purposes, as in the French Third and Fifth Republics or the Southern Democratic primaries.[6]

The significance of all these arguments is limited by the large proportion of state legislators elected from multimember districts (45 per cent).[7] This is offset, however, by the organizing effect on voting choice of the party label. The contest is largely between rival slates, where the competitive logic of the single-member district still applies. All electoral systems discriminate with increasing severity against the second, third, and fourth parties, respectively; but proportional representation is the least discriminatory and single-member districts with plurality elections are the most discriminatory.[8]

Single-member districts and plurality election make the formation of two parties within a given electoral district the most practical way of competing. But what binds these local parties together? Here the presidency as the single major national office and political prize is crucial. Conceivably, ad hoc coalitions of diverse local parties could organize Congress, but the presidency cannot be partitioned like a French cabinet. The presidency is also a single-member district with plurality election in the individual state units and the same logic of competition applies. To be part of the crucial national political activity of nominating and electing the President, the local parties must affiliate with one or other of the two principal national parties. This was demonstrated by the rapid consolidation of voting patterns in the Electoral College from 1792 to 1800 as the Federalist-Republican competition intensified.[9]

The institutional factors, single-member district with plurality election, and the indivisibility of the presidency all combine to provide a persuasive explanation of the origin and maintenance of the two-party system. The crucial point is the handicap faced by a third party in convincing potential supporters that its efforts will be desirable, let alone eventually successful.

The argument that institutional factors favor the two-party system is relied upon heavily and has seemed quite satisfactory. It has an important weakness, however—it rests on the willingness of party leaders and supporters to defer to pragmatic arguments and to coalesce with the more satisfactory of two available parties; but pragmatic politics are not automatic. For example, the political parties of France were as numerous and divided under the Third as the Fourth Republic, even though in the former the election rules were more favorable to a two-party system. Election rules are not the sole influence on party organization, although they are always significant.

The most important reason for the presence or absence of a two-party system is the degree of consensus in a society about fundamentals in social, economic, and political terms. The society must agree upon the goals it wishes, the standards its political, economic, and social behavior should aspire to, and the means permitted to accomplish these. If it agrees on *what* it wants, political parties can divide on *how* to accomplish this, on lesser issues and personal rivalries. Because they are not fundamental, these divisions can permit pragmatic politics and therefore pragmatic coalitions, in other words, the two-party system.

When deep social conflicts and questions of ultimate goals enter politics, effective pragmatic coalitions cannot survive. The ultimate source of the French multi-party system in the Third and Fourth Republics was not election rules, but the multiple divisions between anti- and pro-clerical, between anti- and pro-Republic, and anti- and pro-socialist forces. Since these conflicts cut across each other, the defenders of the Republic were divided among themselves on the Church and socialism, and vice versa.[10] When a fundamental division of national goals occurred in the United States over slavery, the political parties shattered and the Civil War started. From these instances comes the rationale for a one-party system in many new African states that have great potential for internal conflict, especially tribal. It is thought wise not to allow party competition, since this might stimulate a rivalry which could shatter their fragile internal unity. The two-party system is often seen as desirable ultimately but as an expensive luxury at the current stage of development.[11]

When consensus is so broad that it can be easily ignored, then the institutional factors which are so important in influencing a pragmatic political environment can play their role. The root cause of the American two-party system is a broad social, economic, and political consensus, made possible by a liberal tradition, relative economic abundance, and a pragmatic outlook.[12] The immediate causes are the institutional arrangements of single-member districts, with plurality election and the indivisibility of the presidency.

Consensus cannot be assumed as a constant in America. The events of the 1960's severely strained such consensus as may have existed in the past. The anger and bitterness of the 1964 Goldwater campaign were evidence of the substantial numbers of people who had not accepted the New Deal and its successors. The 1968 Wallace and McCarthy campaigns were dramatic challenges to the consensus from the right and left respectively. Just as the national consensus foundered on race in 1860, so today widespread antagonism toward Negroes and urban disorder indicates that many do not accept equality for black people as part of the national consensus. Such dissent encouraged Wallace's third party, especially in the South; conversely, in Lowndes County, Alabama, a black political party was formed outside the existing white two-party system there.[13]

Competition—The Rare Condition

Relatively close party competition is necessary to ensure the benefits of party responsibility, that is, a high degree of popular consultation. The majority party margin must be comparatively thin and uncertain if the threat of loss of office is to be real enough to influence the behavior of incumbents. If the balance is close, the minority party will be motivated to make the effort to capitalize on popular dissatisfaction and serve as an agent for popular consultation. Otherwise, the minority party might adapt itself to defeat by reducing its efforts and seeking rewards in patronage from the majority party. Widespread political sectionalism (regional or local one-party dominance) contributes to the pervasiveness of this problem.

For all its importance, such closely balanced two-party competition is relatively rare in American politics. At the national level, two nearly equal contending parties have existed only at three brief periods: 1796–1800, 1840–48, and 1874–92. At most other times, one party is decidedly the majority party. This was even more evident in Congressional than Presidential elections. Over three-quarters of American Congressmen typically win more than 55 per cent of the two-party vote in their districts.[14] It must be noted, however, that competition can exist even if one party is strongly favored, as long as a significant probability of defeat remains.

In state elections, patterns are more irregular but balanced competition is even more rare. The cumulative impact of the Civil War and the 1896 Bryan campaign made the Republican Party dominant in most Northern states and the Democrats dominant in the South for the first third of the twentieth century. The New Deal realignment of party support enhanced the position of the Democrats in the Northeast in the 1930's and 1940's. Later, the impact of the New Deal on partisan allegiances became more pronounced in the Midwest, in the 1940's and 1950's.[15] In the 1960's, the Democratic attachments of the South weakened dramatically. Recent assessments of the post-World War II period classify one-half (twenty-five) of the states as competitive, and the other half as exhibiting varying degrees of dominance by either the Republican or Democratic Party.[16] This represents a growing trend toward competitive parties at the state level, away from the earlier typical situation of one-party advantage or dominance.

The importance of this lack of competition is suggested by the likelihood that in any given election only 10 per cent of the seats in the United States House of Representatives will be likely to change parties, and usually this is the same 10 per cent.[17] Similarly, in state legislatures most seats are "safe" and therefore popular control through the consequences of general elections is diminished.[18] After the conclusion of nominations by the two parties, 75 to 90 per cent of the officials who will hold elective office in the United States after the coming general elections can be predicted with a very high degree of confidence.

On the other hand, legislative majority control can rest on a swing of relatively few seats, quite often within the range of marginal seats. Thus, the possibility of turnover can be an influence even when it does not occur. Widespread malapportionment of state legislatures before 1962 tended to restrict the possibility of turnover and to reduce competitive pressure. The reapportionment of most state legislatures since then has enhanced competition[19]—the massive turnover in the control of the New Jersey Senate in both 1965 and 1967 being one example. Since the shift of a few officials can create new policy possibilities, the large degree of stability should not mask the consequences of the degree of competition that does exist.

The sources of political regionalism will be discussed in Chapter IV as part of the consequence of partisan identification. The presence of regions or localities of single party dominance does modify the performance of the two-party system. In particular, it provides opportunities for third parties.

Third Parties

The minor parties in America help to further an understanding of the two-party system. The effort required to start and/or maintain a third party is very great and its rewards quite small, as the foregoing discussion has suggested. Their very existence is evidence that they are outside the national consensus that rewards pragmatic two-party politics. This can be illustrated by the principal features of the two prominent types of minor parties which have contested more than a single election: sectarian and state.[20] On the other hand, temporary national third parties can loom much greater on the political horizon, because they represent serious challenges to the existing consensus and may modify it in the long run.

The sectarian third parties are national parties of long duration and narrowly doctrinal emphasis. Examples are the Prohibition or Socialist Labor parties. Their political campaigns and candidacies are primarily mechanisms for propaganda efforts, for instance, the aggressive seeking of "equal time" opportunities on television and radio. These parties persist on the basis of a handful of true believers. They are politically isolated and irrelevant, and serve the psychological rather than political needs of their membership.

The state third parties can boast more frequent electoral victories in the past, but their future is dim. The Farmer-Labor Party in Minnesota, the Progressive Party in Wisconsin, and the Socialist Party in a number of cities have battled on equal terms with Republicans and Democrats. Where successful, the combination of exceptional leadership and a unique ethnic group base has usually been responsible. Over time, however, the impact of competition for the presidency forces alignment with one or the other of the major parties,[21] which is reinforced by the erosion of ethnic group support as it assimilates into the dominant political culture.

New York State provides an exception to the general decline

of state third parties.[22] Here they are favored by a unique provision of state election law which permits joint endorsements of the same candidate by different political parties, the "vote-wasting" weakness of a third party being therefore reduced. The third party can bargain with the major parties for the value of its endorsement. In this context, the third party is acting partly as a political party and partly as an interest group. But the nature of its membership sharply limits the bargaining power of both the New York State Liberal and Conservative parties. Normally, Liberals endorse Democratic candidates while Conservatives would support Republicans, but their capacity to influence those two major parties is limited by the difficulty they have in threatening to support the opposition if their programmatic demands are not met. They cannot easily deliver their supporters to a different major party as a means of protest. This is a greater handicap for Liberals than Conservatives because the highly ideological character of the Conservative Party supporters makes them willing to be "spoilers," thus enhancing the credibility of their threats. Furthermore, the status of these two parties in New York State may be weakened by the recent partial institution of the direct primary for statewide nominations. Primaries reduce the role of a central party organ (the state convention) through which Liberals and Conservatives were accustomed to bargain with Democratic or Republican state leadership, and exclude their registered voters from participation in the crucial nomination process, because voters registered in one party in New York State may not participate in the primary of another party.

The third type of minor party, the temporary national party, has been much more significant in its impact on American politics and the American party system. Parties like the Progressives of 1912 and 1924 or the Dixiecrats in 1948 indicate intra-party conflict and realignment of the bases of support of the two major parties.[23] These third parties can represent either way stations in the realignment of groups from one major party to another, or a temporary protest against national party policy. In both ways, they articulate unsatisfied demands from which the major parties may later borrow the most popular and compatible items, as happened to the Populist demand of 1892 for direct election of United States Senators. They can have long-run influence on the composition, leadership, and doctrines of the major parties.

The 1968 campaign of former Alabama Governor George C. Wallace was a striking example of the impact of a temporary national third party. Both major political parties and their Presidential candidates had to stress "law 'n' order" to match his appeals. The Nixon campaign utilized more gentle but frequently repeated echoes of Wallace attacks on the federal courts, the administration of school desegregation, anti-war demonstrators, and urban disorder.[24] It did this because the partisan attachments of many traditionally Democratic groups (for example, labor union members or more recent immigrants) had weakened under the nationwide Wallace attack on the Democratic Party. Considerable defections from normal Democratic voting provided the new Nixon Administration with an opportunity to build the areas of popular support for the Republican Party. If his administration proves successful in building on that base, 1968 could mark the inception of a major realignment of party support in America.

The Wallace campaign was favored by the twin crises of the Vietnam war and urban riots. Without the doubt, fear, and anger thereby created, George Wallace would have been only one in the series of Southern third party candidacies considered below. His failure to carry any state beyond the Deep South, and the low levels of support elsewhere, were such setbacks that it seems likely only a continuation and intensification of internal disorder could revive the American Independent Party in 1972. Its persistence as a Southern third party is somewhat more likely, however. Moreover, it probably has facilitated partisan realignment in the South by weakening ties to the Democratic Party.

Southern Third Parties

The form of third party with the greatest contemporary relevance is the Southern third party—meaning, the use of third parties and unpledged electors by Southern Democrats to defend their sectional interests on civil rights and related questions. The two tactics are interchangeable because the object is to prevent a majority in the Electoral College for each of the two major party candidates for President. Occasionally, great fear is aroused over the possibility of such a deadlock and its consequences.[25]

These fears focused on the 1968 Presidential campaign of George Wallace, but were somewhat excessive. Many major hurdles must be overcome by the third party strategy. To be successful it requires a close election, some atypical aggregations of Electoral College votes, a willingness of one major candidate and his supporters to set aside the popular vote choice in bargaining, and the willingness of independently elected Congressmen to support the bargain. Close examination of each of these conditions will reveal the low likelihood of such a deadlock and crisis.

Unless the popular vote were close and this fact had been expected well in advance of the election, the effort to create a deadlock would seem futile. However, if the election is perceived to be close, the argument that a third party vote is wasted becomes a stronger one for the major parties. Typically, third party candidates lose support in public opinion polls as Election Day nears because the marginal voter can be more directly influential by voting for one of the two major parties. Consequently, the necessary condition of a close election undercuts the likelihood of a third party vote. For example, Wallace dropped from 21 per cent in late September polls to 13 per cent of the final vote in 1968.[26]

Even if the popular vote is close, the Electoral College normally magnifies that margin. The closest two elections in the twentieth century, those in 1960 and 1968, still resulted in an Electoral College edge of 34 votes above an absolute majority for Kennedy, and 32 for Nixon, respectively. A very atypical, virtually arbitrary combination of regional support would be necessary to achieve the required standoff in the Electoral College that could give 20 to 30 electoral votes from three or four Southern states the balance of power. Even more striking is the fact that the Electoral College provided a more definite decision than the uncertainty attached to the popular count as the nationwide computer tally collapsed during 1968 election night.

Arguments that a shift of about 4,500 votes in Illinois and 23,000 in Texas would have given the election to Richard Nixon in 1960 miss the point.[27] If the appeals and/or conduct of the Nixon campaign had changed enough to gain sufficient additional votes in selected groups to capture those states, these changes would probably have given him additional votes in other states as well. This could have altered the result in other marginal states (e.g., Hawaii) and, more important, reversed the popular vote majority. The electorate is not isolated into state packages, neither are the trends in voting behavior easily isolated. In 1968, this point was even more compelling as similar voters decided the fates of Richard Nixon and Hubert Humphrey in Missouri, Illinois, and Ohio. Any attribute of the campaign or the voters that would have given any one of these states to the Democrats would probably have reversed them all.

The third party strategy requires an intricate balancing act. Just enough support has to be drawn off to balance the two major parties short of an absolute majority. If the third party candidate runs too well, he merely creates a landslide in the Electoral College, as was the case with Theodore Roosevelt's Bull Moose attempt in 1912 or Robert La Follette's Progressive campaign in 1924. Such a third party candidate is obviously significant, but also unsuccessful in terms of the objective of deadlocking the Electoral College. Moreover, because such a third party or unpledged elector strategy usually improves the electoral chances of the majority party which it most bitterly opposes, it misses the object of its protest. The third party destroys the second party's monopoly of the opposition role, and presumably the effectiveness and cohesion of the "anti-" vote which consequently cannot achieve its maximum potential. This strategy is usually directed against an incumbent President, since the acts of the national administration are necessary to heat up and focus local protest. If so, the division of the opposition should merely add to the existing advantages of an incumbent President in seeking reelection.

In 1968, such reasoning would lead to the conclusion that George Wallace hurt the Republicans in the North as well as the South, because in both regions he appealed to opposition to the national Democratic Party, its leadership, and programs. Some opinion poll evidence on the second choices of Wallace voters supported this conclusion.[28] On the other hand, the fact that most Wallace voters were normally Democratic Party voters meant that his voters were probably drawn away from Humphrey. Furthermore, the relatively weak showing of Wallace even in the South meant that he did not cost Nixon too many electoral votes there, but might have hurt Humphrey badly in narrowly divided urban Northern states. Therefore, the Electoral College effect of the Wallace candidancy might have been pro-Nixon regardless of the impact on the popular vote.

Even if the Electoral College deadlock should occur, further problems, not usually considered, would remain. If the election went into the House of Representatives, the Southern members of Congress could not be relied upon to follow the third party strategy. While they might be under local pressure, they also have national government careers to consider. Loyal Democrats in Congress would certainly weigh drastic revenge on Representatives who delivered the White House to Republicans. Therefore, Wallace hoped to achieve his "solemn covenant" before the Electoral College officially voted on December 16, 1968.[29] Whether or not a bargain was struck by unpledged electors in the Electoral College or Southern Democrats in Congress, the legitimacy of the popular vote majority might limit the eagerness of the two major parties to meet Southern terms. A presidency gained at an open sale of the popular choice might have a very short-lived triumph. Deadlock may have only a limited value if the responsibility for bargaining is politically dangerous.

As a means of achieving national political goals, the Southern third party strategy has been uncertain and possibly self-defeating, especially before the 1968 Wallace campaign. So one naturally questions why it has often been supported by a large number of experienced Southern politicians. The answer lies in the fact that the idea of a Southern third party need have very little to do with national politics at all. It can be the expression of the needs of *state* political leaders. It has provided a means to demonstrate white militancy on racial questions and opposition to the national Democratic Party, both very popular stands locally, without the career risks that a decisive and effective step against the national party would require. Joining the minority party of the Republicans could contribute directly to the defeat of the national Democratic Party in the Presidential election, but it would cut the insurgent off from achieving success in state politics. He could not pursue his career in the local majority party but would have to fight the long uphill battle to achieve competitive parity for the Republicans. This was the reason, with one major exception (Senator Strom Thurmond of South Carolina), that Democratic recruits to the Southern Republican leadership have been men either at the beginning or at the end of their political careers.[30] Unpledged electors and third parties meant "safe and sane" revolts with minimum risks and maximum advantage to the state political careers of their exponents, dynamic and ineffectual opponents of the National Democratic Party. They illustrated how the federal system helps to decentralize American political parties.

Nevertheless, the fear persists that the Electoral College will produce an unfair result. While the evidence seems substantial that the plurality victor in popular vote has little to worry about, various reform proposals are continually offered. Two representative types of proposal are the revision of the Electoral College allocation formula, or the discarding of the Electoral College in place of direct election by popular vote in the nation at large.

There is little need to consider the various proposals for revising the Electoral College. Proportional allocations of electors by the popular vote in the state, or distribution by popular majority in each Congressional district, only amplify the possibility of an Electoral College victory without a popular vote plurality. Either of these formulas would have given the election to the candidate lacking a plurality in 1948 and 1960, when the present system did not.[31]

The proposal for direct election of the President has gained in popular approval since state legislative and Congressional reapportionment gained ground.[32] The judicial pressure on Congressional gerrymandering has undercut the defensibility of the large urban state bias of the Electoral College. This urban bias was defended as a compensation for the rural bias of Congress. It is now argued that the reapportionment of Congress requires that the urban bias of the Electoral College be eliminated by substituting direct election. This newer argument neglects the continuing malapportionment of the United States Senate, the lag in House of Representatives reapportionment, and the disproportionate share of long tenure, and therefore power, available to rural Congressmen.

Direct election by popular vote eliminates the uncertainties and complexities of the Electoral College. It penalizes efforts to restrict voting rights in any state by reducing that state's influence on the outcome, and therefore extends majority rule. Regional third parties would be discouraged by eliminating the deadlock will-o'-the-wisp; on the other hand, national third parties without state or regional bases would become more significant and would be encouraged.

To ward against third party impact the American Bar Association proposal, which is a focus of current discussion, would require a runoff election when the plurality winner had less than 40 per cent of the total vote. In fact, this remedy would spread the disease, by giving voting blocs the opportunity to create runoffs and provide bargaining leverage for their support in the second round. The experience with runoff primaries in Southern primaries shows that this device rewards, maintains, and extends multi-factionalism.[33] The Bar Association proposal might weaken the two-party system. A simple plurality system is more likely to produce absolute majorities by forcing groups to coalesce before the single election. Here Schattschneider's concept of monopoly on opposition by the second party creates a powerful pressure toward two-party competition. The 1912 election is the only one between 1860 and 1968 when the plurality winner had less than 48 per cent of the vote.[34] Creating a greater runoff possibility could encourage the persistence of a party such as George Wallace's.

Summary

Competition is critical to the performance of the American two-party system. The centrality of competition rests on its promise to provide the motive which leads political parties to facilitate democratic government by expanding participation, making elections meaningful, consulting popular preferences, and providing a focus for responsibility in government. Nevertheless, evenly balanced competition between two parties is not always found or easily achieved in the United States. The unevenness of party competition and the instability of national consensus limit the fulfillment of the expectations associated with the two-party system and contribute to the existence and impact of temporary third parties. Southern third parties have recently seemed especially threatening to the normal political system, particularly the election of the President; but this problem may be somewhat overstated, especially the likelihood of electoral stalemate.

Paradoxically, the best way to ensure absolute majority rule is to insist on plurality elections. The competitive advantage of the second party over all third and fourth parties in a situation permitting pragmatic politics means that any plurality will approach or exceed an absolute majority. Even the Rube Goldberg device known as the Electoral College is not immune to this logic. However, the national social, economic, and political consensus necessary to pragmatic politics is rare in the world and not always viable in the United States. It broke down over slavery in the nineteenth century, was threatened by insurgency several times since, and is under grave attack from both the right and left in the 1960's. Whether leadership able enough to reconstitute this consensus in the old or a newer, more satisfactory fashion exists will decide whether two-party politics continues to characterize American party competition. More importantly, the survival of the two-party system indicates that basic problems have been solved or ameliorated sufficiently to allow politics to deal with something less than fundamentals.

While the Party Government and Responsible Party prototypes are heavily dependent on competition, the Nonpartisan and Status-Quo positions are respectively indifferent and actively hostile. The Progressive position is in part a response to limitations on party competition and therefore stands midway between these two sets. The mixed nature of party competition in the United States does not support a decided partiality for any of these prototypes. The limited number of closely balanced constituencies does indicate the need for direct voter control outside the parties favored by the Progressives; on the other hand, the turnover in control of office effected by the small number of marginal constituencies does provide opportunities for the operation of the Party Government and Responsible Party prototypes.

The limits on party performance in the United States are not confined to deficiencies in party competitiveness. Equally or more serious are the consequences of the weakness of party organization discussed in the following chapter.

III. the limits on party organization

PARTY ORGANIZATION helps to conduct elections, recruit and select candidates, and mobilize the electorate for a choice. Above all, the continuity of such organization enhances the likelihood that these services will be provided regularly, not just at peak periods of popular political excitement.

Different conceptions of the best ways of achieving democratic government lead to different attitudes as to the appropriate strength for a party organization. One can focus on the competition between parties as the means to achieve democratic government, that is, inter-party democracy. Then strong, effective party organizations would seem highly desirable. If one chose to apply democratic theory to the individual parties, however, then strong party organizations might be a threat to intra-party democracy, which is usually sought by leveling, egalitarian methods reducing the effective centers of influence within the party structure. The question is whether the requirements of both inter-party and intra-party democracy can be satisfied by the same party organization.

One answer is to assert that effective party competition does not require strong party organization. This is the Progressive position. The Status-Quo and Nonpartisan positions, on the other hand, downgrade the relevance of competition and inter-party democracy, and reject strong party organization on those grounds. The Party Government proponents focus on inter-party democracy through competition between strong organizations and usually argue that intra-party democracy is compatible with it. For example, they endorse the notion of a stronger party caucus in Congress capable of serving as a control device for both party leaders and rank and file, which seems a somewhat internally contradictory notion.[1] By placing less emphasis on strong party organization as a means to achieve inter-party democracy, yet wishing to facilitate inter-party competition, advocates of Responsible Parties do not escape this dilemma either.

Actually, internal democracy in political parties may either hinder or facilitate democratic government. The party prototypes differ greatly on the relationship of strong party organization to intra-party democracy. It is these differences which are central to more specific conflicts involving questions of a low evaluation of party organization, the alternative means of recruiting party workers, the choice between the direct primary and the convention for nominating candidates, and the legal regulation of political parties.

Organization—Vice or Virtue?

Party organizations have an inflated and unfavorable image in American politics: they are not as pervasive or as effective as is commonly assumed, nor are they as malignant in their consequences as their Progressive and Nonpartisan critics have often claimed. The gap between common expectations and actual practice is a major theme of this chapter—this gap reflects the impact of reforms inspired by past and current hostility to party organization.

Actually, current political party organizations in the United States are rarely dominant; moreover, they are usually fragmented in structure. Often the only organization in a given community consists of nuclei gathered around candidates for or incumbents in public office.[2] A variety of circumstances may coordinate the efforts of these candidate nuclei, but monolithic machines are rare to the point of being regarded as an anachronism, for example, the O'Connell organization in Albany, New York.[3]

The major reason for the prevalent misconception of party organization lies in the ebb and flow of the development of American political parties. The major American parties progressed toward comprehensive organization following the Civil War, but have declined in organizational effectiveness throughout the twentieth century.[4] The most important implication of this pattern of party development is that the limitation and fragmentation of party organization is a response to the political machine which was the form of comprehensive party organization prevalent in the late nineteenth century. As a result of this reaction, party organization has been undervalued and weakened in American politics.

Americans are hostile to party organization.[5] Their general political attitudes, constitutional arrangements, and specific party legislation all operate to weaken party organization and hamper its capacity to fulfill its potential. American political attitudes, especially individualism and egalitarianism, make the average citizen very receptive to the direct democracy assumptions of the Progressives. He is anti-organization, even anti-leadership; he may go so far as to disparage the relevance of political skills to the conduct of government. Traditional antagonisms toward visible concentrations of power (the visibility often seems more crucial than the actual extent) coupled with the experiences of the late nineteenth and early twentieth centuries reinforced support for the Progressive and Nonpartisan prototypes of political parties. These attitudes have persisted into the middle of the twentieth century. Americans are largely unaware of and unsympathetic to the positive functions of political party organization.

The fragmentation of political party organization is inherent in the constitutional structure of national and state governments. The emphasis on checking and limiting governmental authority expresses itself in constitutional provisions whose impact has been discussed earlier. Federalism further limits the cohesion and organization of American political parties. Because separated branches in both national and state governments create different constituencies for elected executives and legislators of the same party, the legislative party comes primarily from party strongholds, while the executives must appeal to marginal districts. Consequently, conflicts in programmatic priorities are built into each party by separation of branches.

State constitutions often have special features of their own which limit the effectiveness of the minority party. For example, the attempt to isolate state politics from national politics by scheduling state elections in other than Presidential election years has prevented the state minority party from profiting by national trends. In the past, malapportionment of the state legislature by the dominant party prevented popular majorities from being turned into legislative majorities. The long ballot with many elective executives increases the likelihood of divided control when the minority party is gaining support. Electoral victories for the top of the minority ticket are negated by these barriers to equal victories in other offices. Any governor faces the possible partisan or factional opposition of other elective executives and one or both Houses of the state legislature. The possibility of coordinated and responsible party government is further weakened because the most competitive states are most likely to produce divided control and emphasize the differing party factional alignments.[6]

The limits on party organization in recruitment, nominations, and statutory regulation discussed below express this public hostility and reinforce the dispersal of influence within political parties which is aided by the constitutional structure. Moreover, they illustrate the tension between the requirements of inter-party and intra-party democracy.

Recruitment

The character of the personnel of a party organization is largely determined by the incentives offered to work in the organization.[7] The different types of incentives (material, social, and normative) have strikingly different consequences for the cohesion and discipline possible in party organizations. For example, material incentives are often regarded as much more likely to produce cohesive organizations with strong leaders, whereas normative and social incentives are generally regarded as more divisive and conducive to weak and divided party organizations.

Material incentives (job patronage, government favors, even graft) were far more dependable for the purposes of the traditional party machine. The precinct committeeman could do favors for his constituents, place some in minor jobs, and be rewarded himself by a job or help to his business. His following, based on these rewards, enabled the organization to control conventions and primaries for its candidates. Candidates therefore contributed to campaign funds and appointed the organization's men when elected. This tight control over government enabled the organization leadership to punish insurgents and reward supporters and led to organizational discipline and cohesion. The effective coordination and control of officials with constitutionally dispersed authority coordinated public policy and induced interest groups to make substantial campaign contributions in order to ensure favorable treatment. Material incentives in turn generated new resources to maintain the organization.

Material incentives were not without their limitations, however. They could create disunity, as well as unity, in quarrels over distribution of the prizes and control of the organization. They often repelled from party activity those who responded to other types of incentive. Moreover, they were not necessarily used rationally for party purposes, but rather to care for incompetent brothers-in-law or charity cases. Graft, for example, not only created unnecessary liabilities for the whole organization, but was often conducted for private, nonparty purposes.

Patronage and related material incentives are generally harshly judged; for the balance, one should note their more positive aspects. It has been argued that, in some cases, the political machine provided a degree of consistency in public policy by informal coordination of the frequently weak formal structure of American government. Especially at the municipal level, the lack of adequate authority and accountability to the major officials discouraged innovation and invited corruption.[8] Material incentives led people to do the unglamorous drudgery of registering voters and conducting elections, which no one else would do. The extent of "no-show" jobs, inefficient service, and graft depended on the apathy of the public. An alert public forced the machine to be more careful in its appointments and practices. Therefore, it might be said that the cost of patronage was an indirect tax on the nonparticipant in party organization. The less the average citizen was willing to do himself, the higher the cost he had to pay for someone else doing it for him.[9]

The centrality of material incentives to the late nineteenth-century machine was quite clear. Reformers who wished to reduce the party organization's power for evil simply sought to reduce the supply of material incentives. Civil service reform aimed at reducing the number of jobs available, and "nonpolitical" boards and commissions were intended to reduce the authority of the political machine. Reformers sought to deny party leaders any capacity to reward or punish workers; by this means they hoped to erode the discipline of the organization and give others the opportunity to prevail against it.[10] Such a reaction against the corruption, tyranny, and inefficiency possible under boss rule was reinforced by the defection of business groups which had earlier contributed to the party organization. Having received the lucrative franchises and legislation they wanted, these businessmen wished to reduce their costs by not having to continue paying for their advantages in the form of campaign contributions. Their new-found fiscal purity could be protected by a diffuse governmental and party structure.

Civil Service reform thus aimed at weakening the bonds that made party organization cohesive and effective: pull and influence were to be abolished by ensuring the neutrality of government employees. The almost complete victory of the merit system of appointment at the national level has moved at a slower pace in state and local governments, but the expansion has been persistent and permanent to date. First, middle-level positions with easily tested skills were classified, then the system was expanded upward toward policymaking positions and downward toward laboring jobs. In some states, governors can make fewer than twenty appointments outside merit system restrictions. The supply of material incentives has decreased to the point where the traditional urban machine is now almost extinct.[11]

Normative incentives (the satisfaction of ideals and broad public purposes) provide the motivation for amateurs in politics.[12] Recruitment in terms of public policy goals and ideology provides a number of zealous workers but is highly disruptive of pragmatic two-party politics. Dedication to the party program leads to bitter quarrels over the content of that program. A well-defined party position can be exclusive rather than inclusive, a fatal error in a pluralistic and politically apathetic population. Attempts to appeal to marginal voters require a dilution of party dogma that would be opposed by the hard core of party workers. Thus, the internal and external needs of the organization come into direct conflict. Normative incentives limit the flexibility of the organization leadership, because they are not defined by the leaders. They also limit the flexibility of the party system per se, because normative incentives can more easily divide than unite party members.

Social incentives (the enjoyment of participation, sociability) are reflected in the political club as a center of social activity. Especially in urban areas, individual clubs often act as secondary ethnic associations. They provide a place for newcomers to get acquainted, at the club picnic or other fund-raising events which may be a meeting place for young men and women who are single. For many, the activities provide outlets denied in their work or home. Social incentives are a diffuse property of the group and cannot be easily manipulated by the leadership, however. Attempts to use such incentives as a control over members are more likely to disrupt the group and reduce its appeal. Social reasons may prevent the replacement of long-time precinct committeemen who are popular among club members but ineffective in their precincts. The most serious limit on social incentives is the widespread availability of nonpolitical organizations which can offer as good or better opportunities for sociability and participation.

Usually, material incentives are dependent on electoral victory and are therefore a strong motivation for competition. However, division of the spoils of victory can be disruptive. Normative and social incentives stress other considerations—

the ideal or the group—alongside election success. The priority of the ideal or the morale of the group may well conflict with expedient campaign tactics such as the inclusion of antagonistic groups or programs. However, sociability and idealism help to sustain the minority party when it is a weak competitor. In such a situation, material incentives are likely to lead party leaders to an accommodation with the majority, through which they will accept token amounts of patronage while deliberately keeping their party small, so that they hold a larger share of the small pie, as did Southern Republicans in earlier days.[13]

There is an important mixed type of incentive to party organization work, which produces "the partisan," one who enjoys participation in the political game and is intensely loyal to his party. This represents a mixture of social and normative incentives, and attachment to a party label rather than to any specific programs of that label.

The partisan incentive to organization is valuable because it is not heavily dependent on the degree of competition currently available, but is still oriented toward competition generally. In this way, it is far more widely useful than any of the pure types. It enhances party cohesion but does not require dependence and docility toward the organization leadership. Many professional politicians are far more "partisan" than "materialist" and have demonstrated this by putting their own money into politics rather than taking money out. Politics is a popular spectator sport, but it can also be totally engrossing for its participants, regardless of their initial motivation or incentive.

The decline of material incentives and the modest capacity of other incentives to substitute for them help to explain the infrequency of disciplined, cohesive party organizations today. In 1968, Mayor Daley of Chicago certainly made a major contribution toward keeping the stereotype of the machine politician alive, but the discipline of his organization is unique among major cities in the United States.

However, the picture is not uniformly one of organizational decline. The continued slow realignment of parties toward the issue bases of the New Deal has increased the impact and importance of other types of incentive. Amateur club movements based on the growing political participation of the suburban middle class have skillfully utilized both social and ideological incentives; the McCarthy Democrats in 1968 and the Goldwater Republicans in 1964 represented these tendencies. Both these movements captured or established numerous organizations at the local level. Party organization is most significant at this level, a party's effective cadre being composed of its local workers. Consequently, future candidates who wish to enroll their active support must heed their ideological tendencies.

Nomination

The direct primary has replaced the convention as the principal method of making party nominations, because of a concern for intra-party democracy. This change has been criticized for its adverse effects on competition and inter-party democracy. Conventions and direct primaries are both in fact subject to different but significant weakness in achieving popular consultation and majority rule.

The nomination convention of the late nineteenth century permitted the party organization to dominate the selection of party candidates. Precinct caucuses or precinct committeemen selected the delegates to the nominating conventions. The active organization workers and their leaders were thus well placed to control the convention membership at every level. Control of a bloc of delegates permitted access to the bargaining in which a party ticket was completed.

Participation was limited and favored groups with already established access to the organization leadership. The continuity in the organization resisted the easy access of new groups on the political scene and inclined the leadership against candidates who would threaten their control. At the convention, a face-to-face group could consult and conciliate the various factions of the party. Explicit deliberations on the appropriate balance of a ticket on ethnic, geographic, and factional lines was facilitated. Presumably, a collective judgment on the choices needed for general election victory was possible, even though it may not necessarily have occurred.

At the beginning of the twentieth century, however, the convention came under increasingly severe attack. The number of states with competitive parties decreased after the election of 1896, whereas antagonism toward strong political organizations continued to grow. The convention system of nomination favored the machine, and the increased noncompetitiveness of general elections—combined with the strong party identifications of voters in that period—reduced the possibility of effective popular retaliation against unpopular choices made by party organization leaders at the convention.[14] A large number of defectors from strong party ties was needed if the minority party was to win and so punish the majority party organization.

As a response to one partyism, the direct primary allowed voters to select their party's candidates directly. If one party was dominant in a given district or state, the important election choice would be in its nomination election. The direct primary, first tried out in Georgia in 1893, became a major component of Populist-Progressive reform and was widely adopted before World War I. Today, the direct primary is used in all but a few states (Indiana is the most complete exception) for most or all elective offices. In some states, conventions are still used in one of several forms: statewide elective office only (New York and Delaware); combined with the optional possibility of challenging the result in a later primary (Connecticut and New York); or nonbinding preliminary to a direct primary (Colorado, Utah, and Massachusetts).[15] Informal party conventions are used in Wisconsin, Minnesota, and California, and other variants occur in five or six states.

It is important to note that the substitution of the direct primary for the convention was designed to reduce the capacity of party organizations to dominate the nomination process. Less effective party organization was the principal goal, not a byproduct, of this reform effort. The consequences for party organization of this shift from convention to direct primary can be assessed by examining the three presumed democratic benefits of the direct primary. The claims are as follows: "unbossed" selection of candidates; direct participation by the people; and provision of a substitute for inter-party competition.

The attempt to ensure an "unbossed" selection of candidates by eliminating the organization's direct role in the selection of the party's nominee makes the role of leaders less visible and obvious, but not necessarily less influential. Candidacies are not the products of spontaneous creation or simple consensual adoption by the voters. Who, in addition to the candidates themselves, initiates and promotes individuals for the nomination? The answer in many cases is the party organization, where it has been able to cope with the impact of the direct primary. Only now the organization may be less visibly responsible for its choices and less answerable for them to the public. If the organization is not effective, influence passes to those who can provide the campaign workers, funds, and publicity needed for victory in the primary. Responsibility for a candidate can hardly be traced by the voter and the voter is far less able to repudiate a group if it changes the candidate it runs. Consequently, the visibility and continuity that make responsible parties possible is reduced.[16]

The Progressive's focus on the evils of the visible party organization led him to neglect the problem of controlling the less visible organizations which might replace it. He failed to recognize that leaders are needed for candidate selection. Not only is this inevitable, but as long as responsibility to the public can be enforced, it has positive advantages. An organization is likely to require that a candidate work up through the ranks, thereby enabling him to gain experience and adjust to the complex realities of American government before running for a major office. The Progressive's concern with bossism obscured the question of the actual focus of responsibility for initiating and promoting candidacies. Thus, the voter had the appearance of choice but might know very little about what was actually happening.

The direct primary involves greater numbers of people than conventions but is often subject to significant biases. In two out of three non-Southern gubernatorial primaries, less than 35 per cent of the eligible registered voters cast ballots.[17] As little as 10 per cent of the electorate can therefore control the outcome of important primary battles, and does so with great frequency. Given the relative importance of primary elections in areas with noncompetitive general elections, this low level of participation contradicts the view held by advocates of direct primaries that conventions are a restraint on eager citizens.

Much more important than the low level of voter turnout is the potential inherent in direct primaries for misrepresenting party opinion. The turnout at a primary does not represent a cross section of party support; those voters who are less partisan are less likely to vote in the primary than the deeply committed. This means that the groups whose support is least certain and most necessary in the general election are almost unrepresented in the primary electorate. Among the strong supporters of the party, the turnout is relatively higher in areas where the party has a majority; here the primary result for local offices *is* a guarantee of election. Where the party is in a minority, however, the primary turnout is very low because of the low value of local nominations. In Massachusetts, for example, over 50 per cent of the Democratic primary votes come from Boston, but that city contributes only 30 per cent of the party's general election support. Democratic votes from the rest of the state are needed to reduce Republican pluralities so that the Democratic plurality in Boston will provide a statewide majority. While a candidate can be nominated on Boston appeal alone, tickets composed solely of Boston Irishmen lack the appeal necessary for statewide victory.[18]

Convention leaders were more concerned with tickets balanced on ethnic and geographic criteria. The fact that conventions generally corresponded more closely to the distribution of party support in the general election enabled them to reflect the statewide variety of groups and interests, to the degree that these groups participated in the party organization. Also, the convention gave partisans who were outnumbered in their own constituencies an incentive to maintain local party organizations in order to control delegates to the state convention. The abolition of conventions has led to the decay of minority party organization and an increase in the number of noncompetitive constituencies.[19]

The direct primary produces an imbalance between party strongholds and areas of minority support, and between deeply partisan participants and marginally partisan nonparticipants. These differences are enhanced when one party is weaker overall than the other. Then the minority party has to reach beyond even its nominal supporters to gain victory. Its own primaries can be dominated by voters very different in attitudes and social characteristics to those voters needed to gain victory in the general election. In fact, the electorate in primary elections may become so different from that in the general election that the minority party finds it difficult to present candidates who can appeal to both.[20] For example, the Democratic Party in New Mexico suffered a serious handicap in 1968 from a state ticket chosen by primary voters that overrepresented the Mexican-American minority in the state; this probably contributed to their defeat by a narrow margin on Election Day.[21] In contrast, a party convention provides a confrontation and the opportunity to make rational assessments of the candidates needed for general election victory. Such rational use of the convention is not of course assured, but the direct primary has no conscious deliberative mechanisms at all because of its fragmented distribution of influence and its favoring of atomistic individual decision-making.

Other consequences of direct participation are reflected in the appeals used to gain the nomination. The candidates must make themselves known to an apathetic electorate and differentiate themselves from their opponents. Therefore, a dramatic slogan and/or personality are tempting approaches, as also is an emphasis on divisions within the party. A frequent tactic in primary campaigns is to exploit the popular antagonism against party organization. People can be distracted from other issues by a successful attack on the opponent as the candidate of the "bosses." The antagonism against party organization, coupled with the decline of material incentives, makes unlikely any coordination of the various primary races. The candidates for each office run separately, requiring a great duplication of effort and money. This enhances dependence on those who provide campaign funds.

The direct primary can provide only a partial substitute for inter-party competition, considerably short of the responsibility and coherence provided by a two-party system. The multi-factional or "every man for himself" situation prevailing in most constituencies gives the voter few if any cues by which to assess candidates and their performance. The continuity of a party label provides a bench mark around which the voter can accumulate experience and form more reliable judgments as time passes. Multi-factionalism, on the other hand, provides no fixed organization to give a candidate blame or credit. If an individual is discredited, his backers can continue their policies behind a new name. The anonymity and transferability of campaign financing puts limits on the degree to which such backers must be accountable to the public, even though the candidate is heavily dependent on them for having adequate funds. The rarity and incompleteness of even the most fully developed bi-factional system of competition in existence, that of the Long versus anti-Long forces in Louisiana, demonstrates the small likelihood of development toward an effective substitute for two-party competition. Even in Louisiana, local contests are not consistently tied to state-wide races, and coalitions are unstable between the first and runoff primaries.[22]

Moreover, the direct primary tends to confirm and strengthen the majority party advantage and to delay a return to competitive parties. The direct primary penalizes loyalty to the minority party by emphasizing the majority party primary as the center of political choice. The prime asset of the minority party is its advantage as the most effective opposition. Opponents of the incumbents can maximize their strength by rallying behind the largest opposition party.[23] But the direct primary breaks this monopoly on opposition, giving dissenters another arena in which to compete. Opposition is divided and the appeal of careers in the minority party further reduced. Men beginning careers in politics are tempted to the majority party even if they are more sympathetic to the minority party. Thus, the minority party organization declines because of lack of interest, workers, and candidates. This further reduces its value as an opposition and leads more individuals to participate in the majority party. A reinforcing vicious circle is established within the minority party and handicaps its efforts to profit by favorable political events. The tradition of Republican Progressives prevented Midwest Democrats from capitalizing on the New Deal realignment until after World War II, when a new generation without strong Republican identification entered politics, long after Republican Progressives had lost control in their own party.[24]

The direct primary does achieve, in part, the expectations of the Progressive reformers. It has done so at the expense of the coherence and effectiveness of party organization. Political bossism of candidate selection is less frequent and effective, although this is also a result of the decline in material incentives which made the traditional machine possible. Popular participation in nominations has been widened but in an uneven manner. Direct primaries do provide an opportunity for successful opposition to incumbents in one-party communities; on the other hand, the direct primary may siphon off dissent from the minority party and make balanced two-party competition less probable. The direct primary enhances openness and flexibility in political parties at the expense of coherence in party organization. Dissent can be more easily articulated when party organization is weak.[25]

As a response to these weaknesses of the direct primary, there is increasing interest in and use of the pre-primary convention and the challenge primary. Either formally or informally, a screening and deliberative process with visible responsibility for party candidates has gained importance in a number of direct primary states. The convention is rarely definitive in the nomination process, but it provides a corrective for the weaknesses of the direct primary. In convention states (Connecticut and New York), a challenge primary is now available as a check on leadership choices.[26] Party organization is encouraged; broader segments of the party are represented; and better balanced, coordinated, and competitive tickets are selected. The encouragement of leadership and organization is balanced by control over abuse of such leadership through the openness and flexibility of the following primary. It is an excellent compromise between the popularity of the direct primary and the needs of effective party organization and competition. Moreover, it is an effort to satisfy the requirements of inter-party democracy (served by responsible party leadership and competition) and also of intra-party democracy (served by popular control over nominations).

Regulation

Because of the centrality of nominations to party function and structure, the single most significant law affecting party organization is the specification of the type of nomination procedure required. Other elements of the legal structure are also influential, however, including state election law and the regulation of campaign finances.

American election law has represented an expression of popular distrust of party organization. Originally, party organizations were treated as private associations, but increasingly their operations and structure were defined, specified, and restricted by law. The changes were consistently negative in character, designed to eliminate past abuses, frauds, or errors by restricting the choices and procedures that could be followed. As a consequence, party organization became highly formalized and reduced in flexibility and adaptability.[27] When this process was carried to the extreme in Wisconsin and California, the party organization was rendered inoperable and had to be abandoned in favor of informal private associations which performed the party organization tasks, for example, the California Republican Assembly or California Democratic Councils.[28] The process had gone full circle and demonstrated the importance of the functions performed by party organization in one guise or another.

Another consequence of the negative attitude of election law has been that high concern for fraud in registration and voting has made voting more difficult in the United States than in most Western European countries. There is considerable evidence to suggest that the relatively low voting turnout in the United States is very largely a result of complex residence, registration, and balloting procedures rather than of a lower level of interest in politics, or a lower sense of citizen duty.[29] For the most part, American election law is a carefully prepared bastion against a long-deceased foe, although some suspicion of Chicago and Texas elections does persist.

The very complexity of election law does allow the party organization some advantages. The direct interest of organization regulars in the details of election law gives them the edge on intensity of activity in its formulation and a high degree of expertise in its use. Insurgents and amateurs are often defeated by flaws in their nominating petitions or an irregular use of party organization rules. The party organization also provides the workers who carry out the bulk of electoral administration. Bi-partisan election boards, composed of organization regulars, direct the process, and the selection of the clerks and judges can be an advantage, even without fraud, in a primary fight. Discretionary decisions on who is properly registered, unconscious errors in tabulation, and the monetary reward of the day's pay all accrue in favor of the incumbent organization.[30]

Campaign finance regulation is essentially negative. The prime motivation is to limit rather than provide opportunities for party organization. Political puritanism, rather than common sense, prevails. Operating on the same logic that produced the Eighteenth Amendment and Prohibition, it is decreed that less money should be spent on political campaigns. To implement this notion, reports of campaign expenses are to be submitted, and relatively arbitrary limits are placed on the amount any candidate or organization can spend. On the whole, it is appearances rather than the reality which is improved. To the limited degree that such laws are enforced, they lead to creation of innumerable campaign committees. Each committee can spend up to the limit, increasing the amount of legal expenditure but further fragmenting party organization. And the regulation of primary elections is usually even more scanty. The impact of these reforms, especially the limits on spending by formal party organization, is to disperse influence in the party even further, and to limit the capacity of the party organization to coordinate campaigns. Fund raisers in these chaotic circumstances become independent powers rather than agents of the organization.[31]

Almost uniformly, party organization is hampered by the formalization, complexity, and rigidity of state election law. Organizational flexibility and innovation are inhibited. In many states the formal shell has to be shed and ignored for parties to be able to function at all. Thus, internal democracy is not much enhanced and participation by voting is actually restricted by the elaborateness of registration procedures.

Summary

The limited capacity of party organization to recruit reliable and effective workers, the hazards of the direct primary, and the extent of formal regulation all reduce the possibility of a political machine in the United States today. Party organization persists only to the degree that it can successfully compensate for the impact of the constitutional tradition of dispersing authority, civil service reform, the direct primary, and detailed election law.

The restrictions on party organization generally serve to open it up and to facilitate participation; they usually support intra-party democracy, or perhaps anarchy in extreme cases. They do handicap inter-party competition, however, by weakening the minority party's capacity to recruit workers and candidates and to make appropriate nominations. The recruitment process for the minority is likely to throw up materialists who take majority party patronage, party groups that exclude needed support in order to maintain their sociability, and ideologues who lead the party away from the political middle ground and voting majorities. The direct primary will permit and encourage the selection of candidates appealing to the hard core, who thus narrow rather than widen party support.

The adoption of anti-organization reforms was sponsored by the Progressives and by adherents of the Status-Quo and Nonpartisan prototypes. On the other hand, most of the reforms desirable to reinforce the Responsible Parties and Party Government prototypes run counter to prevailing opinion on party organization and political parties. For Responsible Parties or Party Government to function, the regulation of party structure and finance must be more permissive, partisan activity more favorably regarded, and party leadership more conspicuous and effective in the nomination process. Although these necessary reforms are not very drastic, they will obviously be difficult to achieve.

A failure to appreciate the value of organization is a crucial and continuing problem of American politics. The limits on party organization in recruitment, nominations, and statutory regulation express the public hostility and reinforce the dispersal of influence within political parties facilitated by the constitutional structure. Organizational activity is only part of the range of partisan activity, however. A fuller explanation of political parties must also include a consideration of nonorganizational partisan activity, since to understand the scope and impact of political parties we must reach beyond mere organization to the reaction of voters to party labels. It is partisan identification which lends the necessary continuity, coherence, and influence to political parties. The next three chapters trace this factor in voting behavior, political campaigning, and government, respectively.

IV. voters and partisanship

VOTING IS an action important to democratic theory because it functions to support democratic government. As the means whereby citizens approve or disapprove past acts of government and select leaders and officials, it facilitates popular choice. The potential decisions of voters also influence other mechanisms of government because officials not directly elected must take past or future voting decisions into account in their actions. Thus in many ways voting facilitates majority rule and popular consultation, provided that the political parties organize electoral choices so that past acts can be approved or disapproved and make public officials sensitive to voting decisions.

What is required of the voter to fulfill these functions satisfactorily? What kinds and levels of knowledge must he have? What concerns and criteria must he bring to bear on his choices? These are the questions that need to be answered to ascertain the quality of American voting behavior for the purposes of democratic government.

The characteristics of American political parties depend heavily on the characteristics of the American electorate. To which issues or candidates is it most likely to respond? How does it form its voting choices? The debate on party prototypes draws heavily on varied assessments of the significance of ideology, the rationality of partisan allegiances, and political interests of the average voter. Each prototype visualizes the voter differently. The Progressive assumes that voters are highly rational and well informed. Nonpartisans essentially agree, but see partisan labels as capable of blinding the electorate to its own interests. The Status Quo places a relatively low value on the rationality of the voter's choice in order to have political parties enhance stability. The Responsible Party credits political parties with the capacity to organize and to enhance choice of the most appropriate admixture of policies and candidates. Party Government assumes that the most rational reflection of voter attitudes is a choice between two distinctive party programs.

Recent studies of voting behavior have sharply revised and expanded our knowledge of the American electorate. Most important, many popular "common-sense" notions about voting have now been discredited. Some interpretations stress the irrationality of voting behavior, while others confidently specify the voters' reasoning in highly rationalist terms. However, the strongest barrier to understanding how and why Americans vote comes from within the observer. The temptation to generalize from one's personal perceptions entails three overlapping biases: obviously, in the first place one is more likely to perceive what suits one's own preferences; a second, somewhat more subtle bias stems from generalizations from a biased sample—here, the sociological tendency for friendship and contact with people of similar status and attitudes guarantees that available opinion is selective and nonrandom. The third facet of bias is the least obvious and the most troublesome for a person involved in politics and trying to understand it. There is a great gap between the attitudes and concerns of those involved and those who are apathetic toward politics. The active analyst or participant in politics is necessarily unrepresentative of the larger share of the population and electorate.[1] All three biases listed above should caution the reader not to rely too heavily on his personal perceptions of voting behavior.

What are the important perceptions which influence American voting patterns? How are candidates and political parties known and evaluated? These questions will be dealt with next because the answers help to illustrate the relationship of political parties both to voting and to the larger governmental process. Voting identification with one of the two major parties is the focal point of this analysis. If we start with the attitudes most relevant to voting choice, the significance of partisan identification is readily apparent. The nature of such partisan identification and its development is then followed by tracing the relation of partisanship to public policy attitudes and to alternative bases of voting choice, in particular social class. All these findings challenge typical perspectives on the American electorate and highlight the role of partisan identification as a means of organizing voting behavior.

Perceptions of Parties and Candidates

Political perceptions reflect both predispositions and the impact of new events. Loyalty to one political party, or various acquired social characteristics (such as income, occupation, or educational attainments) can bias one toward a particular choice; this is a psychological predisposition. However, new political events can reshape the voter's perceptions of political parties, issues, and candidates. During a campaign existing predispositions and new events must be taken into account equally, since changes in voting choice from one election to another exceed those in party loyalty or socioeconomic status (SES).[2] The predispositions do not therefore explain all change.

Six attitudinal dimensions have been found to be highly predictive and explanatory of Presidential voting choice.[3] They are (1) evaluation of the Democratic candidate; (2) evaluation of the Republican candidate; (3) evaluation of group benefits by party; (4) domestic policy issues by party; (5) foreign policy issues by party; and (6) party performance as manager of government. No single dimension is sufficient, but by using the responses of voters interviewed on all six dimensions, analysts can predict a voter's choice more successfully than his own preelection self estimate.[4] When these attitudes are consistent in direction, the choice is simple. When they conflict, the voter is under cross pressures and is slower in deciding, more likely to vote a split ticket, more indifferent to the outcome of the election, and less likely to vote at all.[5]

These dimensions help to establish the importance of party loyalty in voting, since shifts on four dimensions are directly related to the evaluation of party. However, changes in candidate evaluation also contribute to the election result. These two different types of dimensions are not equally involved in changes, but rather have different roles in long-term and short-term voting behavior.[6] An examination of these differences illustrates the particular contribution of party loyalty to voting behavior.

Political parties are known and evaluated by the public on the basis of sources remote from the present time, with substantial roots in social groups, and highly resistant to change. The Democrats are typically seen as the party of war, the South, low income groups, the New Deal, and prosperity. Republicans are considered the party of peace, Reconstruction, businessmen, and depression. These attributes are not new or rapidly changing, because the social groups which initially held them conserve and transmit them to succeeding generations.[7]

Moreover, the image of the incumbent party is more likely to change than that of the opposition. The low level of interest and knowledge about party politics and public events means that the actions of the ins are more likely to be known and evaluated than the words of the outs. The incumbents will have a sharper image than the outs, who profit more by the errors of the ins than by any alternatives they may offer.[8] In 1968, the lack of any discernible new program in the Republican campaign was a tacit acknowledgment of this factor.

Since 1945, the Democrats have been favored by popular evaluations of their party on domestic policy issues and benefits to social groups. The content of these issues and group alliances dates back to the New Deal and is consistent with the urban, working-class, and liberal orientation of its policy and programs. This evaluation shows less a personal commitment to a position on any specific issue than general confidence in the party's intentions and efforts. The Democrats are seen as the party of the "working man" and of "good times" economically.[9] Barry Goldwater sharpened this attitude in 1964 by seeming to reopen such settled issues as social security. By doing so he revealed the popularity of the basic New Deal reforms, which has been affirmed in numerous public opinion polls and was repeated conclusively in the 1964 election.[10] In 1968, however, the Republicans were able to downgrade such traditional issues by introducing the issue of "law 'n' order" and thereby reducing the Democratic domestic policy advantage.

Under Eisenhower, the Republicans had an advantage on two other dimensions, foreign affairs and management of government. Needless to say, the Korean war and influence-peddling scandals in the Democratic Administration were a considerable Republican asset here. Although the 1964 Goldwater campaign placed Republicans at a disadvantage on both counts, in 1968 the Vietnam war and the urban crisis restored foreign affairs and management of the government to their earlier position as issues benefitting the Republican Party. The association of Democratic administrations with wars throughout the twentieth century reinforced their partisan disadvantage on foreign policy.[11] Furthermore, incumbent administrations have built-in liabilities in responsibility that give their opponents an edge in public assessment of the parties as managers of government, since attention to politics is greatest when and where things are going wrong, rather than in the successful areas.[12]

Compared to the evaluation of candidates, the other four dimensions of voting attitudes (group benefits, domestic policy, foreign policy, and government management) remain relatively stable. The variation in electoral advantage is four times as great on the candidate dimensions as on all the other four dimensions combined.[13] Candidate evaluation is therefore an important source of short-run change in election outcomes.

Candidate appeal is not simply equivalent to personality. Eisenhower was a big asset for the Republican Party in 1952 and 1956, but so was Richard Nixon in 1960. Eisenhower was more likable, but both he and Nixon were favored by the electorate because of their broad experience in matters the public regarded as crucial to the performance of Presidential tasks. Eisenhower was not perceived merely as a war hero. During the postwar period, he had combined military with diplomatic experience as commander of the North Atlantic Treaty Organization; the Korean war was seen therefore as a task for which his skills and experience were highly relevant. Nixon's travels and career also seemed a valuable attribute to the American public. Whatever their merits, Kennedy's foreign policy critiques gained far fewer votes than his espousal of Democratic domestic policy and his mobilization of Democratic partisanship.[14]

Johnson was the only Democratic candidate in the period from 1952 to 1968 to gain voter support by being favored over his Republican opponent in candidate evaluations, and this was primarily an anti-Goldwater response. Here again, the unusual character of the Goldwater campaign violated the typical pattern, which stresses voting choice as more a response to the incumbent party and candidate. There was a 13 per cent increase in the Democratic percentage of the two-party vote from 1956 to 1964 because of the change from an Eisenhower-Stevenson to a Goldwater-Johnson comparison.[15]

The impact of a given candidate is a result both of his actual properties (record, positions, and decisions) and his image or style. And both are filtered or perceived by the voter through the biases of his own party loyalty, religious identification (1960), and general political attitudes.[16] "Attractiveness" is not solely a property that can be manipulated by the candidate and his campaign staff. Existing predispositions cannot be so easily disregarded, and these predispositions are not always apolitical but are often directly relevant to the choice being made.

Since the end of World War II, the components of voting choice most directly related to party have shown relatively little variation and have generally favored the Democratic Party; but candidate components have been highly unstable and have varied widely. There have been cliffhangers and both Republican and Democratic landslides in the last six Presidential elections. In the short run, candidate and issue evaluation supply the dynamics of electoral choice.[17] The stimulus of new candidates and issues, and the rapid turnover in objects to be evaluated, generate change from one election to the next. In any given election it is the political party that provides the continuity, the baseline for electoral competition.[18]

The way in which this continuity and electoral stability are provided point up the major contribution of political parties to American voting behavior. Political parties organize and relate voting decisions to government action, and the linking concept here is partisan identification.

Partisan Identification

The pervasiveness of partisan identification by voters is what makes it so significant. The stability of a voter's allegiance to one or the other of the two major parties is directly related to the likelihood of voting and to voting preferences. It also promotes widespread and informed participation in the political process. While voting decisions are much more than the simple reflection of partisan ties, partisan identification is the single most important factor influencing individual voter decisions.

The tie between the voter and the political party is the voluntary psychological identification with the party by the voter. Unlike many Western European parties, one does not become a dues-paying member of a formal organization in America. Nor is active participation in party work a necessary requirement for being considered a member. Membership is without obligations and is at the discretion of the individual. One is what one says he is. No one has the authority to withhold membership or require obedience from a member. The decentralized structure of American political parties prevents the existence of any groups with such authority.

Partisanship is thus a voluntary, individual psychological attitude, a willingness to identify one's self as a Republican or Democrat. However, this is not equivalent to voting Republican or Democrat at all times. To define party membership in terms of voting record is to blur the distinction between the psychological attribute (partisan identification) and one of its behavioral consequences (a strong tendency to vote for the candidate of a particular party). The conditions under which a self-identified Democrat votes for a Republican candidate are important since the relationship between partisan identification and voting record is only approximate. Because voting behavior is not tightly determined by partisan identification it is crucial to understand the dynamics of this relationship.

Partisan identification among the electorate has been polled quite regularly and with increasing accuracy for the last twenty-five years or more. The basic pattern was relatively stable in the 1950's and 1960's, fluctuating only a few percentage points up or down (Table II).

TABLE II

VARIATION IN PARTISAN IDENTIFICATION: 1952–68*

	High	Low	Median
Democratic	51	43	46
Republican	32	23	27
Independent	30	15	22
Apolitical	10	1	4

* SOURCE: Simplification of data presented by Survey Research Center, *The Distribution of Party Identification in the United States* (Ann Arbor, Mich.: The University of Michigan, Mimeograph, November 1968.

It has been found both possible and useful to rank the actual intensity of an individual's partisan identification. Democrats and Republicans will readily classify themselves as "strong" or "weak" in their partisan attachments, and strong partisans differ in a consistent fashion from those who regard themselves as weakly or mildly partisan. There are also differences among Independents, which can be divided into three categories: "leaning Republican," "leaning Democratic," and "neutral." Similarly, these slight distinctions are reflected in voting tendencies.[19] As a group, however, self-identified Independents differ markedly from partisans in their behavior and attitudes. Again, the voluntary identification is a useful index to behavior.

The stability of the percentage shares of partisan identification would seem to imply that partisanship is highly stable. However, only the net change between parties has been small during the period being examined. There is considerable change in intensity of partisanship over time. Campaigns increase the relative percentage of strong partisans and after the campaign is over many voters slide back to being weak partisans or Independents leaning in one direction. Moreover, equal shifts from one party to the other or to Independents, or vice versa, would cancel each other out leaving no net changes, despite a great deal of redistribution of voters. This is, in fact, what happens. The exact percentage is difficult to establish, but at any given time roughly 20 per cent of the electorate has shifted from one party to the other or to the Independents, or has moved away from the Independents to one of the major parties. Roughly half of this change has occurred in the last four-year period between one Presidential campaign and the next.[20] The electorate is like a pack of cards that gets *partially* reshuffled from one election to another. Strong partisans provide relatively stable cores, but the weak partisans and Independents are in flux. This permits more movement and potential for change than the raw figures would imply.

The distribution of partisan identifiers implies a Democratic Party edge much greater than the usual election returns, because the Independents do not normally break evenly between the two parties but favor the Republicans. A better estimate of the balance of partisan identification is the concept of "normal standing division." As propounded by Philip Converse, the partisan balance is best expressed by balancing all short-term influences on electoral choice so that neither party is favored. All other things being equal, the resulting abstract electoral choice should reflect the normal division of party support. While the concept and the procedures used to compute it are controversial, it does yield, at the very least, a plausible "guesstimate" of basic long-term partisan identification advantage. Normal division was computed to be 54 per cent Democratic and 46 per cent Republican.[21] This is roughly equal to the vote for Democratic candidates for Congress from 1952 to 1960, the same period as that from which the normal partisan division is calculated. Furthermore, this advantage remains constant under varying assumptions of voter turnout.[22] The 54–46 per cent split between the Democratic and Republican parties is a figure worth keeping in mind. It is a meaningful, if not precise, indicator of the Democratic Party advantage in national politics. The Republican Party starts every election with a substantial handicap in partisan identification.

Partisan identification is important for its direct and its indirect impacts on voting choice. Perhaps the best way to demonstrate this is to contrast partisans (those who identify with either of the two major parties) with Independents (nonpartisans). Political independence is quite fashionable in current American political attitudes, and an explicit element of the Nonpartisan and Progressive image of the voter. It is contrasted to "blind partisanship" and stresses the slogan of voting for the man, not the party. But the 20 per cent of the electorate which calls itself Independent contains many in the process of changing allegiance, or concealed partisans. For example, the voter who has always "chosen the man," can often wind up with a series of choices like Hoover, Landon, Wilkie, Dewey, Eisenhower, Nixon, Goldwater, and Nixon.

Moreover, the image of the Independent as the superior, rational voter is nonsensical. On every criteria of voting performance that can be devised, the Independents are vastly inferior to partisans. Independents have poorer knowledge of the issues and candidates, have a lower interest in the campaign and its outcome, make their choice later and with less rationale, and are less likely to vote at all. The more partisan the voter, the more likely he is to have the positive attributes of the good citizen voter. Independents are the least-informed, rational, and participant part of the electorate. Some miniscule minority of "true independents" who fit the popular stereotype may exist, but they are not numerous enough seriously to modify the weak qualifications of Independents as voters.[23]

Independents are not the same as "switchers," however. V. O. Key stressed the rationality of voters who switched from one party's candidate to the other in successive elections.[24] He found that switchers were relatively well informed and were voting in ways consistent with their policy choices. Nevertheless, Independents are not redeemed by this evidence, because party identifiers often vote for candidates of the opposition party. The difference between switchers (who have changed their voting choice between elections) and Independents (who have demonstrated an attitude toward partisan loyalties) illustrates the need to distinguish between psychological identification and current voting choice in establishing party membership.

The primary reason for this reversal of expectations is that partisanship gives a voter stronger motivation to participate and therefore a greater probability of being informed. The correlation between voter quality and partisanship could also be explained by suggesting that informed participation leads to partisanship. This alternative explanation is unlikely as a major cause, since partisanship develops earlier than participation in or knowledge about politics.[25] Either way, partisans are underrated as voters.

While the perceived closeness of the contest increases the likelihood of voting by the more strongly partisan,[26] partisan motivation is not the sole explanation of the decision to vote. Of four dimensions of political involvement (interest in campaign, concern over outcome, feeling of political effectiveness, i.e., political efficacy, and citizen duty) only the last, citizen duty, has a strong relation to the decision to vote. Half of those voters with low interest in the campaign, little concern over its outcome, or little confidence in the effect of their vote do vote anyway. Americans are so innoculated with citizen duty that they will vote without interest, concern, or confidence[27]—Table III. There are five times more unmotivated voters than highly motivated nonvoters. Independents with

TABLE III

POLITICAL INVOLVEMENT*

	Percentage Who Vote
High on all 4 dimensions	96
Low on all 4 dimensions	22

* SOURCE: Angus Campbell, Philip E. Converse, Wallen E. Miller, and Donald E. Stokes, *The American Voter* (New York: John Wiley and Sons, Inc., 1960), p. 107.

high citizen duty are the blindest segment of the voting public. They are motivated to vote but not to make an informed choice.

Voting turnout raises a number of questions related to partisanship. One persistent issue is the party orientation of nonvoters. A myth, widely believed by conservative Republicans, maintains that because large numbers of conservatives are offended by look-alike liberal Presidential candidates, they stay at home in protest. Actually, these hordes of social-welfare conservatives do not exist. In every election those social strata most likely to support conservative ideology (the highest levels in status, income, and education) are the most likely to vote at rates exceeding 95 per cent. For example, the 1952 Republican Presidential nomination pitted the conservatives supporting Robert A. Taft against the more liberal segments of the party supporting Dwight D. Eisenhower, in a bitter battle lost by the conservatives; yet in the following general election, Taft supporters had a 94 per cent turnout rate, while only 84 per cent of the Eisenhower enthusiasts voted.[28] The higher propensity of higher status groups to vote contributes heavily to the more conservative character of state and municipal government, which have lower overall voting turnouts than occur during national elections.

Liberal Democrats have an alternative myth. Because voting rates become lower as one moves down the scale of socioeconomic status (SES), and the Democratic vote increases with lower SES, they conclude that the nonvoters are disproportionately Democrats. Public opinion polls during the Roosevelt Administration seemed to confirm the notion that higher turnouts among present nonvoters would aid the Democratic Party. It seemed rational that low income nonvoters would be similar in party preference to low income voters. However, this plausible notion has come to grief with more thorough analysis. Philip Converse has found that the standing division of party support does not depend on the size of voter turnout. Rather, as turnout declines, Independents are more likely to drop out than partisans, due tc lower motivation. Although, among partisans, Democrats are more likely to drop out than Republicans (because of weaker indoctrination in citizen duty in the lower income groups[29]), the loss of Independents limits the Republicans because of their edge in this category. This counterbalances their relative gain in higher turnout among partisans, and the net result appears to be little different from that expressed by the normal voter turnout.

Moreover, the Democratic hidden-vote hypothesis ignores the differences between voters and nonvoters. Consider the following polls of nonvoters in a year of Democratic victory (1948) and of Republican victory (1956), in which the poll results follow the victor (Table IV). The nonvoter has low involvement in politics and fewer fixed and reinforced attitudes about political issues, candidates, and parties. Therefore, he is easily changed in his preferences by broad popular shifts. He is susceptible to a "bandwagon" appeal but has no political

TABLE IV

POST ELECTION PREFERENCE OF NONVOTERS*

	1948 %	1956 %
Democratic	82	28
Republican	18	72

* SOURCE: Campbell, *et al., The American Voter,* p. 111.

effect because of his failure to vote. This point will be confirmed later by the data on levels of sophistication in assessing public policy issues. It reflects one of the many ways in which those with low involvement differ from those who are highly involved in politics.

Parties directly stimulate voting turnout by their organization of political choice, as demonstrated by the jumps in voting turnout when the Democratic and Whig parties were organized.[30] The dramatic shifts in political party alignment have been marked by jumps in voting turnout, more the result of new participants than conversions (Table V). These figures reflect the reorganization of the American electorate. Al Smith in 1928 began to build an urban Catholic working-class base for the Democratic Party, and the New Deal added Black and Jewish voters to the coalition. Note that the 1932 election (a temporary anti-Hoover vote) involved less change in turnout than the elections before and after it, which reflected more durable changes. The election of 1940 confirmed the pattern which the 1944 and 1948 elections followed. Since new stimulus was lacking, turnout after 1940 declined absolutely

TABLE V

TURNOUT IN PRESIDENTIAL ELECTIONS, 1920–40*

Year	Percentage of Resident Population 20 or Over Voting
1920	40.3
1924	41.5
1928	49.9
1932	51.2
1936	55.5
1940	57.5

* SOURCE: U. S. Bureau of Census, *Historical Statistics of the United States, Colonial Times to 1957* (Washington, D.C.: U. S. Govt. Printing Office, 1960), p. 682 for voting turnout; and U. S. Bureau of Census, *Statistical Abstract of the United States,* Vol. 52 (1930), p. 11; Vol. 62 (1940), p. 2; and Vol. 87 (1966), p. 5 (Washington, D.C.: U. S. Govt. Printing Office) for population data. The estimate is a gross one, but hopefully sufficient for the purposes intended.

and relative to population, despite increases in the number of potential voters. The turnout in absolute numbers did not exceed that of 1940 until 1952.[31]

Partisanship also modifies the effect of laws aimed at facilitating or reducing partisan voting. The strongly partisan voter is likely to vote a straight party ticket regardless of ballot form, but Independents will have a tendency to vote straight party on a single choice ballot and split their ticket on a multiple choice ballot. They tend to follow the path of least resistance. Formal political institutions have the greatest impact when the relevant attitudes are least intense. Since many voters have low involvement, election law can be a significant influence. The highly motivated voter is not strongly affected, but election law can modify the choice pattern and the decision to participate of those who are mildly partisan or nonpartisan and weakly motivated to vote at all. Election law is significant but selective in its impact.[32] Progressive and Nonpartisan reform thus has the ironic consequence of being most effective on the voters most remote from these prototypes' ideals.

The indirect effect of partisan identification through voting turnout and election law is a powerful influence on the rates and pattern of voting. Partisan identification also acts more directly on the voter by modifying the political attitudes and assessments which shape the candidate choice. Partisanship can be an important opinion-forming agency, since it creates a perceptual screen through which the performance and characteristics of the two contending parties and candidates are evaluated. A Democrat thinks more highly of his party's performance in foreign policy or managing the government, and is more likely to detect the virtue of its candidate, because such perceptions confirm the correctness of his past decisions. The consistency of partisan identification with political evaluations is enhanced by the prior development of partisanship.[33]

One should not overstate the significance of partisan identification. The six evaluative dimensions discussed earlier are more immediate to the actual choice and more variable than partisan identification. Attitudes can and do conflict with partisan identification, for example, Democrats who feel that Republican foreign policy performance is better. Votes often conflict with partisan identification for any given election, for example, anti-Goldwater Republicans. Half the variance on these six dimensions controlling voting choice is explained by partisan identification. It is the single most important variable, as stressed, but not the sole one.[34]

During campaigns these attitudes and partisan identification interact. Realigning elections may shift the attitudes so dramatically that the partisan identification will also shift to become more consistent with them. It is likely, however, that the important changes occur between elections. For reasons that will be discussed more fully in Chapter V, election campaigns tend to reinforce existing attitudes, rather than leading to conversion to new beliefs and perspectives.

Perhaps the best measure of the relative influence is when the six political attitudes governing voting choice conflict directly with partisan identifications. The relationship then depends on how well developed (articulated, informed, and intense) the political attitudes are (Table VI).

TABLE VI

PARTISAN IDENTIFICATION AND POLITICAL ATTITUDES OPPOSED*

	Well-developed Attitudes %	Poorly-developed Attitudes %	None %
Percent voting with partisan identification	20	47	75
Percent voting against partisan identification	80	53	25
(N)	(143)	(164)	(36)

* SOURCE: Campbell, *et al.*, *The American Voter,* p. 142.

When the voter has well-developed and negative opinions on various aspects of current party and candidate attributes, he will vote against his partisan identifications four times out of five. When these attitudes are so weak as to provide no guidance, partisan identification is controlling in three times out of four. Moreover, partisan identification enhances the likelihood that these attitudes will be consistent and agree with partisan identification, because of perceptual screening.

Partisan identification is a very strong psychological force, but it contends for influence among other relevant political attitudes. Only when these competitors are exceptionally weak or absent does partisan identification act directly and decisively on voting choice. Usually, it is a mediating variable on these attitudes which directly control current voting choice. Partisanship provides a consistency and intensity in voting behavior lacking in the less partisan and Independent voters. How this psychological attribute arises and the consequences of the way in which it develops form the focus of the remainder of this chapter.

Development of Partisan Identification

Three major social processes contribute to party identification by the individual voter. Major historical events create crises in party support, realigning the electorate primarily by redistributing the partisan allegiance of various social groups. These allegiances are then inherited by individual voters before voting age through the partisan biases of their immediate social environment, which are shaped by group memberships. This initial affiliation is reinforced by partisan perceptual screening of political events and by continuity in group memberships. The importance of these factors is further demonstrated by the limited impact of social class on American voting behavior.

The major current bases of party support stem from the realignments caused by the Civil War and the Great Depression, and to a lesser degree from the impact of the William J. Bryan campaigns as Democratic Presidential candidate in 1896 and 1900. Not only were these periods political upheavals at the time, but the partisan divisions of these generations were carried over and show up in the long-run political geography of many states. The same counties have supported the Republican Party for three and four generations.[35] This is seen most strikingly in relatively rural counties with stable population composition. The initial division in the community may rest on much earlier party alignments or on its pattern of settlement by ethnic or social groups closely allied to one party or another. For example, rural Indiana counties north of U.S. Highway 40 are usually Republican, while those south of the highway which divides the state into two parts are usually Democratic. Northern Indiana was settled in waves from Whig and Republican New England, while southern Indiana was populated by migrant farmers from Democratic Kentucky, Virginia, and Tennessee.[36]

These striking patterns are made possible by the relative homogeneity and intimacy of the small communities involved, which inhibit the development of the opposition party. The dominant party can monopolize the channels of political recruitment and advancement and represent the consensus of the community. Initial patterns provide it with a preponderance in the immediate social influences on those born into the community, which thus helps to maintain the party's advantages.[37]

The minority party can survive even such a disadvantage, however. If the minority party supporters have a drastically different ethnic and social background, they will be relatively isolated from contacts with the majority party supporters and will be reinforced by a tendency toward associations with their fellow minority party members.[38] For example, in the heavily Republican farming area of Champaign County, Illinois, there are isolated, traditionally Democratic precincts which contain the area's concentration of German Catholic farmers.

Political regionalism is also enhanced by other factors. The federal system provides political payoffs for isolating governmental units from larger trends. Local political strength is protected by setting it against the larger community. Rural versus big city political conflicts are quite valuable to Republican and Democratic Party leaders in their respective strongholds. By stressing their role as spokesmen and defenders against the "evil" city politicians, rural Republican leaders can discredit any Democratic threats to their local control. Similarly, urban Democratic leaders can defend their power by linking local opposition to their party with greedy farmers who hate the city and its people. The country-city fight, which is basic to the politics of so many states, is a profitable game for party leaders in their strongholds. Whipping up hysteria on this point is an ace-in-the-hole for party leaders threatened by an upset. The usefulness of this conflict gravely hampers those party leaders, especially gubernatorial candidates, who have broader concerns and need broader support. Their need to play down these conflicts leads them into disagreement with their own party stronghold leaders. This difference in strategy enhances the likelihood of intra-party conflict on regional lines, as those seeking statewide leadership are more concerned with those areas where their party is closely competitive or in the minority.[39]

The extension and reinforcement of partisan allegiances to larger, but relatively homogeneous political communities by the processes mentioned above can reduce the impact of class or socioeconomic status on party support. The resulting heterogeneity of fellow partisans can enhance the possibility of limiting the distinctiveness of a party program.

Party identification is an individual psychological attribute with deep social roots. Development of a partisan affiliation occurs early in the individual's socialization into political life. Except for the vaguest orientation toward government and governmental authority, and particularly the President, partisan identification is the earliest political attitude developed.[40] It therefore dominates the processes of political socialization.

A person usually begins to regard himself as a Democrat or Republican before reaching voting age, often by his early teens. This identification reflects the partisan affiliation of his parents. The greater the agreement between one's parents in direction and intensity of partisanship, the stronger and more stable one's partisanship will be, because the partisan character of the child's immediate environment (his parents, their friends, his playmates, and the particular community of residence) is normally controlling. Since the likelihood is great that all of these will share similar SES attributes, most will be of the same party, reinforcing a favorable evaluation of that party. A party is evaluated well before one has any considerable amount of interest in or knowledge about politics. The "good guys" and the "bad guys" are largely defined by early associations: only later does one acquire a rationale for this choice.[41]

A later increase in detailed political knowledge has important effects. Partisan affiliation can screen and distort political events in a manner favorable to the party, which reinforces partisanship; but this process is not total and political attitudes inconsistent with partisan affiliation can develop. This creates the discrepancies discussed in Table VI and permits flexibility in election outcomes.

The development of partisan identification in childhood gives social groups a major role in maintaining the stability of partisanship. If, for historical reasons, a group has distinctively supported a political party, someone born into this group will grow up in an environment with a strong partisan bias. Group membership is always a powerful mechanism for creating social values; "bloc" voting is a popular term which reflects group-party alignments that stand out in voting returns. This phenomenon is easily misunderstood, however. No group is 100 per cent Democratic or Republican, because each person has a number of group memberships, some of which might lead to support of the competing party; for example, an individual may be both Roman Catholic (which would predispose him toward a Democratic vote) and a businessman (which would predispose him toward a Republican vote). Many of the most distinctively partisan groups are so because of overlapping and reinforcing group memberships. A manual worker in an Eastern city is likely to be a Democrat, because he is also likely to be a labor union member and a Catholic.[42]

Moreover, the capacity of a group membership to create a strong partisan identification is not easily reversible. The group's leaders cannot "deliver" their membership to the other party, because the distinctiveness of the group means that its strongest identifiers are also the most partisan and the most difficult to shift. The least partisan of the group's members are also likely to have the weakest identification with the group and be the least susceptible to its influence.[43] Partisanship derived from group memberships becomes an independent force that retards group realignments, as can be seen by the fact that well-to-do Irish Catholics vote more heavily Democratic than Protestants of comparable income and occupations. Group influences reflect the heritage of past party differences and help to maintain partisan differences.

Historical alignments, socialization, and group processes all work to limit social class as an explanation of voting behavior. Social stratification of course is an objective and social economic reality, with only an indirect political significance. Variation in SES is not consistent or clearly defined in all regions and circumstances in the United States. American pluralism and egalitarianism lead to a reluctance to use the terminology of status and class and make perception of such status unclear. This is reflected in the difficulty of finding "objective" measures that differentiate political and social attitudes clearly.

If "class" means something more than a number of related group memberships, it must have psychological reality and motive power to the individual. There should be "class consciousness," a subjective perception of one's self and others of sufficient significance to influence evaluations and choices. This class consciousness depends in turn on the extent of "class polarization," the perceived conflict between one's self and others of a different status.

The difference between objective measures (social strata) and subjective measures (class polarization) is shown by the greater predictive value of self-assessment over objective assignment of the individual when the two are in conflict. A person who is objectively a member of the working class, but regards himself as middle-class, is much more likely to vote Republican than those co-workers who are self-identified as working-class.[44]

Class polarization varies in extent and intensity. It reflects the party past and is most marked in strong partisans. For example, a strong concentration of polarization is found among union members and businessmen. In recent times its peak was in the 1948 campaign, which stressed the contrasts of the New Deal.[45] The variation in polarization over time prevents social stratification from being consistently predictive of voting behavior. For this reason, sociologists who emphasize class and status variables have had only limited success in analyzing voting behavior.

A political party can have a social class base of support without class consciousness. The class may have been politically relevant at one time, and may be so again in future campaigns, without being consistently influential. It is useful to remember that representatives of all social strata or classes are distributed in both parties in varying proportions, and that class polarization is limited even at its peaks.

Because of its dependence on complex and repetitive social processes, partisan identification grows over time. Repeated voting for one party increases the probability of voting for it in the next election. The psychological commitment represented by voting, plus the screening effect of partisanship, reinforces a favorable attitude toward one's party.[46]

The persistence of partisan affiliation is also favored by the lack of conflicting stimuli. One's family, friends, and coworkers are likely to have the same party identification. Low social mobility would keep a person in the same environment that shaped his parents' affiliations and his own early inclinations, whereas the highly mobile individual is more likely to shift parties since he drastically changes his immediate social environment. A man from a working-class background who is college educated and undertakes a career in business may move from a Democratic to Republican identification, but this is not certain, because early influences are not easily overcome.[47]

Shifts from one party to another are more often the result of social forces than personal influences: the ratio between social and personal motivations for shifting is roughly five to one.[48] Personal influences are most marked in women, who often shift to their husband's affiliation if there is a conflict. This is a result of social norms which restrict the legitimacy of a role for women in politics.[49] Social forces operate more effectively when geographic and SES mobility modify the individual's environment by reducing social reinforcement for his current affiliation. This would be so, for example, for an individual promoted from a unionized industrial job and a working-class neighborhood to foreman and a middle-class neighborhood. The increase in social polarization between Republican and Democratic Party supporters caused by the New Deal realignment has increased the impact of SES mobility on party affiliation. Furthermore, the changing American society has produced drastic increases in geographic mobility, reducing the role of a stable, homogeneous community in restricting partisan competition and stimulation. Even so, changed social or economic status has only a modest direct influence on partisan identification or voting choice. The frequency discussed conversion of Democrats when they move to Republican suburbs has been demonstrated to be vastly overrated.[50]

The early development of partisanship in the immediate social environment of the individual shows why very radical political events are needed to realign political parties. Short of the Civil War and the Great Depression, most realignments have been partial and slow. For these reasons, shifts in the partisan balance have taken greatest effect at the weakest link of the processes which form partisanship, the first vote.

The voters with the least partisan identification are those who are voting for the first time. The young or new voter has no psychological investment in past choices and is likely to have greater geographical and SES mobility. Because the new voter has less developed preferences and involvements, he can be more easily converted or recruited by the immediate campaign and/or choices. This is why realigning elections are marked more by a considerable expansion in the voting turnout than by conversion of the existing electorate, a factor that is also shown in the greater percentage vote for the winner among young voters than the total electorate in most recent Presidential elections.[51] Political experience is more likely to lead to strengthened partisanship than conversion. Perceptual screening and stability of status in later years is most likely to confirm to the individual the wisdom of his earlier choices.

The development of partisan identification is clearly a complex process, based on the common impact of usually parallel factors: family, neighborhood, classmates, fellow workers, group memberships, and community patterns. The process is subject to great variation, but it can produce the high degree of continuity in partisan identification which is so distressing to its critics. This continuity further complicates the task of building stable third party support, since a generation of crisis elections might be necessary before social processes would sufficiently reinforce identification with a third party.

Partisanship is irrational because it is based on old quarrels and issues—or so it has been argued by many critics. Thus it may distort and confuse current policy debate by preventing the appropriate realignment of political forces. The merits of this argument can best be evaluated by considering the relation of partisanship to public policy divisions, which also involves us in the way in which various policy attitudes are related and organized, or the extent of ideology.

Partisanship, Public Policy, and Ideology

The main problem in analyzing the relationship between public policy issues and partisanship is the great difficulty in connecting them overtly. For an issue to have any effect on voting choice and the evaluation of political parties, three conditions in the voter's perception must be satisfied: (1) the issue must be recognized and known in some intelligible form, (2) it must arouse at least some feelings pro or con, and (3) the voter must perceive one party as closer than the other to his own position. These conditions might seem relatively easy, but in fact they are not readily met.[52]

Familiarity with an issue is not easily deduced from the extent of newspaper coverage it may have received. For example, at the height of the debate on the Taft-Hartley Law in 1948 (which President Truman had made a focal point of his reelection campaign), one-third of the electorate did not know anything about the law, and another third had no opinion. Furthermore, familiarity varies from issue to issue, and the more specific the question, the less the knowledge. Quite often the relationship to government will not be perceived. On almost any issue at least one-third of the public will not have either an opinion on the issue or an awareness of its connection to public policy.[53]

The effect of an issue on the voter is important because information is not readily retained where personal values do not promote interest and because more familiarity does not lead to a position on the policy question. The degree of intensity of feeling on an issue does not depend on its intrinsic importance but on those value preferences and priorities of the individual voter which it involves. Such value preferences and priorities are crucial, highly variable, and not easily predicted. They are especially hard to anticipate if one attempts to impose one's own standards about what is important. This has been the source of much silly analysis of the American voter and his opinions. The gross overrating of the significance of the issue of "Communists in the government" in 1952 is an example of this; although widely assumed by analysts to be a major issue, subsequent research has proved it was among the minor issues in voter concern.[54]

Even if the voter is aware of an issue, and has an opinion, this may have no implications for a particular vote or partisan affiliation. The voter must connect the opinion with a party position favorable or unfavorable to it. However, the perceptual screening of his own partisan identification, the ambiguity of party position created by pluralistic, fragmented party leadership, and/or inadequate information may prevent the voter from perceiving differences between party positions. If so, his opinion has little relevance for his voting decision. This ambiguity and distortion make it possible for him to reconcile his policy position and party support, even when they are actually in conflict. To continue the Taft-Hartley example, most voters in 1948 saw their preferred Presidential candidate in agreement with them on this issue, regardless of his actual opinion. Thus, 40 per cent of the Democratic voters who were for the Taft-Hartley Act thought that President Truman favored it, even though he had made opposition to it the keystone of his campaign![55]

The difficulty of satisfying all three conditions (issue familiarity, issue intensity, and perceived party difference) suggests some important limitations on the impact of a new campaign issue or of the campaign itself. Long-established controversies are more likely to contain the necessary familiarity, intensity, and partisan differences. New issues have to arouse great intensity, as the Vietnam war or the issue of "law 'n' order" did in 1968, before they can become major electoral influences.

Voters do perceive general differences between the major parties and their greatest consensus is on the position of the Democratic Party, which is described in terms of New Deal linked issues.[56] The party images are a product of national issues and the national party positions. Public consensus about party positions on public policy is vague, and breaks down considerably when relatively specific issue positions are in question. The heterogeneity of party leadership and party loyalties tends to obscure differences, thereby creating a congruence of personal and party position in the individual voter's perception where it does not exist in actual fact. However, a realistic general public perception of Democrats as the pro-labor and social welfare party and Republicans as pro-business and more *laissez faire* on social legislation still underlies public responses.

A more detailed examination of the relationship of various discrete public policy attitudes to each other leads to very surprising results. People do not connect individual issues in a way that might be assumed to be "normal" and "rational." Only certain domestic issues invoke consistent, interrelated responses. Often, issues are treated in isolation. Equally in foreign policy, opinions on one item will not carry over to a seemingly similar question.[57] As a result, public policy preferences are only partially ordered and integrated. Thus the required level of abstraction which produces that especially elaborate, wide-ranging, and coherent structure of attitudes termed "ideology" is decidedly uncommon. Among the discoveries of those engaged in public opinion research which support this assertion is the relative willingness to pay taxes among upper income groups that are opposed to expanded social welfare programs, whereas lower income groups wish expanded social welfare programs, but are much more resistant to higher taxes. In terms of liberal or conservative ideology, these are contradictory attitudes on the part of both groups.[58]

The relation between foreign and domestic policy attitudes is also difficult to reconcile with stereotypes. Internationalists are as likely to be conservative as liberal on social welfare questions. Foreign policy opinion is not only unrelated to domestic policy opinion but is also independent of party preference. Therefore, the parties are limited as mechanisms of popular consultation on foreign policy, a source of great frustration to supporters of Senator Eugene McCarthy for the Democratic Presidential nomination in 1968. This insulation of foreign from domestic policy is explained by the strong correlation of an interventionist or internationalist attitude with higher levels of education, which correlates with SES and social welfare conservatism.[59]

Domestic policy opinions do, however, correlate strongly with party preference and are consistent with party images. Those who take a more "liberal" position on social welfare questions are more likely to be Democrats, and vice versa. The electorate has partisan preferences and domestic policy positions that are *consistent with,* though not necessarily determined by, a party system organized on a conservative versus liberal basis.[60]

Obviously, there is no need to assume that the distribution of party supporters is the direct result of the ideological characteristics of the voter, since domestic policy attitudes are only loosely structured and unevenly distributed between the two parties. Again, the tendency to impose the "logical" perspective of the observer on the average voter should be avoided. Limited self-interest can explain the results, without assuming an ideological motivation. The contradiction between tax and social welfare positions is logical for the lower income voter who wants the program but is more closely pressed by tax increases. The position is inconsistent from a larger frame of reference, but not for the man who reacts to each issue individually. This self-interest explanation is demonstrated by the high social welfare support sources of low status Republicans and the low scores of high status Democrats.[61]

Attempts directly to assess the degree of ideology in the electorate reveal much about the misconception of its role. Ideology is common among élites which are highly involved, informed, and sophisticated about their political participation. They are more likely to organize their attitudes into a relatively consistent ideology. They also would tend to discuss politics with people similar in these characteristics. Consequently, their immediate experience and attitudes lead them to find ideology very common. However, on all the dimensions relevant to politics and voting, they are extremely atypical. The average voter has low involvement, little information, and small concern about politics. He has little reason or opportunity to develop a sophisticated and elaborate (that is, ideological) perspective on politics.

The levels of issue sophistication of the American electorate have been most fully analyzed by Angus Campbell and his associates, whose results demonstrate the limits of ideology as follows (Table VII).

The few ideologues are supplemented by those whose perceptions of issues make partial use of ideological terminology, although not consistently or clearly. Group benefits involve the largest group of voters, but with varying levels of sophistication. Only the upper third of this classification perceives its group interest as conflicting with another group, and the lower third's group reference is vague and broad. Whether the nature of the times is regarded as "good" or "bad" depends on the conditions in the immediate environment of the voter, whether he and/or close friends and family are secure in their jobs and neighborhoods. It is largely a vague feeling of the situation. Seventeen per cent of American voters fall below even this classification.[62]

The percentage allocations to the various levels need not be regarded as fixed. If sustained for a considerable period of time, a sharpening of political conflict in America might move more voters into higher levels of group benefit sophistication and shift the issueless into at least a "nature of the times"

TABLE VII

1956 VOTERS AND LEVELS OF CONCEPTUALIZATION*

Level	%		
A	15	Ideology	3½%
		Near-Ideology	12%
B	45	Group Benefits	
		Conflict seen	16%
		Single interest	18%
		Shallow	11%
C	23	Nature of the Times	
D	17	No Issue Content	
		Party	3½%
		Candidate	7%
		No content	3%
		Unclassified	4%

* SOURCE: Campbell, *et al.*, *The American Voter*, p. 249.

response; yet the 1964 election, with all its stimuli to ideology, did not noticeably increase the proportion of ideological voters.[63] Shifts in relative proportions will probably not occur rapidly, although good arguments can be made for a long-term upgrading of levels of sophistication with trends toward more education.

Summary

The conflict between the expectations of the typical political observer, who is highly motivated, and a voter's actual response to public policy issues and ideology underlines the truth of this guideline for understanding the American electorate: "Hypotheses that seem reasonable to the sophisticated analyst and which are borne out on sophisticated subjects may have no relevance whatsoever for nine-tenths of the population forming the mainstream of the electorate."[64]

Because the studies relied upon are largely based on Presidential elections from 1948 to 1964, extrapolation of these results to other elections and periods must be made cautiously. Nevertheless, the elements of political choice do provide some persuasive clues for other elections. Indeed, the relative difficulty of making up impact with candidates or issues below the floodlit stage of Presidential campaigns points to a far greater role for party identification and evaluations of party performance there. This notion is supported by the agreement between Congressional voting and the normal standing division of the vote which was discussed earlier.

Voting is a choice made within a political and a historical setting, political because of the response to governmental events and performances, and historical because of the relevance of major conflicts and alignments of the past. Within both settings an individual's psychological self-identification with a political party becomes a pervasive factor, influencing his perception and choices.

An attempt to apply these findings to the broader questions of the American political process raises some deeply disturbing issues for democratic government, especially for the key role given to elections. Supporters of the Progressive, Party Government, or Nonpartisan prototypes of parties expect and/or require voters to be rational, well informed, and highly concerned with their choices. American voting studies appear to present the voter as almost completely lacking in these qualities, and thereby to challenge the value of elections, as understood by those who support such requirements for voters.[65]

The following chapter will focus on the analysis of campaigns and elections and draw on the more positive implications of the voting research summarized here.

V. campaigns and elections

AMBIGUITY in democratic theory over the purpose of campaigns and elections arises from two different interpretations of the appropriate use of government power. Those who desire active, innovative government want the electorate to take an active role in formulating public policy during the campaign and election period. Those who focus on the more negative aspects of government power emphasize a restraining role for the electorate.

Advocates of Party Government want the campaign period to provide ample opportunity for policy debate, so that the election may result in a mandate for the policy of the victorious party. The Progressives also want campaigns to provide policy debates as the basis for an electoral mandate, but do not rely on the party as the mechanism for this process. Supporters of the Status-Quo and Nonpartisan prototypes believe that elections are not competent for this purpose, and use this failure as an argument against political parties and majority rule. These critics of democracy stress the limitations of elections, because of lack of competence in the electorate, while many of democracy's most fervent supporters insist on the competence of the electorate and the wisdom of election decisions. If elections are to be evaluated on these grounds, clearly we must be concerned about the nature of electoral behavior and the level of issue awareness of the voting public.

Democratic theory also supports a rival tradition of thought as to the appropriate function of the electoral process, however. This views elections as an instrument by which the electorate protects itself and places a check on government action.[1] Because democratic government was not initially conceived as positive and innovative, but rather as a means of checking arbitrary government, its key goal was responsibility and control rather than policy accomplishment. The Responsible Parties prototype is relatively sympathetic to this conception of elections. The performance of American political parties in campaigns and elections as considered below should suggest which of these two conceptions of elections is more relevant for the United States.

The variety of campaigns and elections in American politics is so vast that a full coverage would exceed the scope of this chapter; here we shall simply summarize the basic features and variations crucial to analysis of political parties. The common dimensions of campaigns are treated first, followed by a discussion of the distinctive attributes of legislative campaigns and elections. Next, Presidential candidacies are traced from the pre-convention phase through the national convention and the campaign itself. The concluding section considers the more general attributes, functions, and performances of campaigns and elections.

Campaigning

H. L. Mencken defined election campaigns in America as: "A deafening, nerve-wracking battle to the death between Tweedledum and Tweedledee." Skepticism about both parties and their rhetoric can lead one to see little significant difference between the parties; in addition, certain basic conditions of the campaign situation have led the parties to exaggerate some differences and minimize others.

The resources required for campaigning include workers, staff, and money. Workers register and canvass the voters and get them out on Election Day. They bring out audiences for campaign rallies and distribute campaign literature. A skilled staff is needed to plan and conduct the campaign, write the speeches, and schedule the use of the candidate's time. Since party organization is increasingly less able to supply the workers and the staff, different appeals and more money must substitute for the face-to-face contacts with the electorate which were made possible by traditional party organization. These pressures and trends toward more professionalized and specialized campaign staffs (with, for example, a greater use of public relations agencies) are limited primarily by the financial costs involved and by resistance from the traditional party organization participants.[2]

The organization of campaigns mirrors and even exaggerates the general decentralization of American political parties. Each candidate usually has his own staff and overall coordinating efforts are often nominal. Only in the strongest party organizations, such as that of Connecticut, are the campaigns at even a single level of government jointly run and financed.[3] The crucial ingredient is the financing, which is the most difficult to centralize because of the campaign finance laws. The supervisory role of national and state party committees is usually limited to disbursement. The funds they spend directly are devoted largely to the leaders of the ticket; other candidates have to fend for themselves.

This arms-length arrangement of financing is often reinforced by the variation in expectations for victory. The favored candidate may well separate his campaign from that of a fellow partisan who is expected to lose—running away from the head of the ticket was not new in the Goldwater campaign; Democratic Senators did it to Harry Truman in September of 1948, and Republicans did it regularly to the ticket leader in FDR's campaigns.

Party fund raisers gain considerable influence from these arbitrary campaign finance limitations and the general fragmentation of party organization. They are the middlemen between major contributors and party leaders, often serving as chairmen of the campaign finance committee for the candidates or the party.[4] A concerted boycott by potential sources of funds has terminated some campaigns and careers before they reached the public. Senator Hubert Humphrey could not raise the necessary minimum to wage an effective campaign for the presidency in 1960; his efforts were fatally handicapped by lack of staff and the need to spend campaign time raising funds.[5] But the role of money in campaigns is often overrated. Money alone is not enough to win. If the candidate can raise the minimum necessary to wage a campaign for a given office, the difference in the funds available to the two candidates will not decide the victor.[6] If a candidate is strongly favored to win, he can raise money more easily than his opponent; his larger campaign fund therefore only reflects the expectation of victory rather than being a cause of it.

The recent proposal to institute an income tax checkoff to finance national campaigns would have given considerable resources to the national party committees and so enhanced their influence. One reason for its defeat in Congress was a concern to maintain the autonomy of the Congressional campaign committees and the campaign organizations of individual Congressmen. Furthermore, this proposal ignored the more serious problems of campaign finance in the states and cities where dependence on a few large contributors is far more likely.[7]

In planning campaigns, situational limits, group and geographical targets, timing, and themes all come into consideration, but the actual carrying out of a campaign can seldom be as rational as its planning. The hectic pace of activity gives disparate elements of the effort their own momentum. Coordination suffers under the pressure of immediate needs and decisions, and an ill-considered response to individual events of the campaign and the opponent's efforts can easily divert the best-laid strategies.

Attempts to get objective information on the level of success of campaign efforts and to remedy their weaknesses are often frustrated. The headquarters staff has its loyalty to the candidate, and/or its operational responsibility, which biases it against perceiving its candidate's weaknesses or those of the campaign plan it helped to develop. Reports from field workers are also subject to the need to defend the effectiveness of one's own performance and these reports are sifted through many hands before reaching the candidate. Crowd reaction, based on rallies packed by loyal supporters, is the most deceptive, since the partisans are often most appreciative of speeches that are quite unappealing to the vitally necessary marginal voter.[8]

For these reasons, public opinion polls have gained great popularity as a campaign planning and checking device. Virtually all other feedback has a tendency toward "echoes," that is, a bias in favor of candidate performance and current strategy. Hopefully, the poll may be more objective in assessing possible strategies before the campaign begins and in testing progress during the campaign. Polls can give systematic and sensitive information, if carefully used, whereas the intuition of even the most experienced politician often rests on faulty assumptions about the electorate drawn from his own concerns and fears (the difficulty of inferring from atypical personal experience was demonstrated repeatedly in the last chapter).

While public opinion polls can indicate the current split in voter preference between candidates, this is their most trivial aspect. Much more useful questions will probe the candidate's image to the voter, what the public likes and dislikes about his personality, career, and campaign. The voters who are most undecided can be located more precisely and the issues of greatest concern highlighted. The reaction to various possible campaign strategies can be tested by hypothetical questions. All these items would be useful in pre-campaign planning, while later polls could assess the effectiveness of various efforts and dictate changes in emphasis (and even develop into a simulation of hypothetical possibilities and appropriate responses).[9]

All this is not to say that the polls will necessarily reveal surprising new truths, but they may create some barriers to simple delusion. If nothing is changed by polls, they still provide reassurance. At the least, they may prevent panic reactions to new events and support consistency in campaign efforts.

The advantage of intuition over polls is cost. It is hard to cut corners on polling, and a cheap poll can be worse than none at all because the biases of a poorly handled poll are every bit as misleading as intuition.[10] Polls vary in quality, depending of course on the intelligence of the questions asked. (For example, Abraham Ribicoff almost lost his bid for the United States Senate because of the overconfidence generated by a poll taken before his 1962 campaign. Connecticut voters were asked for an opinion of him, not whether they would vote for him, and a good opinion was considered equivalent to a committed vote.[11]) Moreover, the low salience of politics means that responses will often be vague and uninformative. The electorate is not articulate enough to be precisely analyzed.

Polls are not the magic tool that some popular novelists like to assume, neither are they the ready means for unscrupulous image manipulation. The candidate's record and personality are not easily made over. Strategies demanded by the people may be out of the question because of previous commitments or the nature of party support; for example, knowing the popularity of New Deal measures could not have changed the Goldwater campaign strategy or the candidate's views.

The hardest part of campaigning is actually reaching the voters. The rallies and speeches affect only the most committed, who are willing to attend. These efforts do not give the candidates new votes, but rather inspire campaign workers who will reach unattached voters. This is why the themes of campaign rallies and most speeches are highly partisan in tone, since that is the most relevant appeal to the special audience these occasions provide. When the speech goes on radio or television and the audience is broadened, the partisanship must be correspondingly muted.

In one sense, much of the money spent on campaign literature, handbills, billboards, and similar items is wasted, since it is usually too poorly designed to be very effective. Only when it is drastically simplified and intelligently distributed can it have persuasive impact. However, these items must be bought and distributed for the sake of campaign worker morale. The fact that they are expected would lead campaign workers to believe that a campaign was in trouble if they did not appear. Also, they have some value as a prop and an information reminder for the campaign worker on his door-to-door visits.[12]

The great growth in mass media campaigning persuaded many to believe that television could displace the organization effort more or less completely, but some years of experience and research on this point have led to a lowering of expectations. The highly motivated voter is the most likely to respond to the mass media message, but he is also the least likely to be converted against his existing inclinations. Since he is likely to be partisan, he will most effectively attend to and perceive information supporting his existing preferences.[13] Consequently, the principal effect of mass media campaigns is to reinforce existing preferences and activate partisans to efforts of their own. This is quite valuable for the campaign leaders, and the skillfulness with which existing preferences are reinforced and partisans mobilized is crucial to a successful effort. But it discourages issue innovation, in favor of a more skilled manipulation of the existing issues. The success of a campaign is obviously enhanced by controlling the range and priority of issues discussed. If the campaign discussion can focus on areas where the party and its candidates are favored by existing predispositions, then the campaign will be successful.[14] For example, "law 'n' order" and Vietnam provided the Republicans with a better situation in 1968 than had been created by the discussion of nuclear weapons in 1964.

Consequently, the use of television and radio has shifted from the thirty- or fifteen-minute speech to the five-minute trailer and the one-minute spot announcement. The apathetic voter will not sit still for politics, but a one-to-five-minute "pitch" is more likely to be endured. The shorter spots can be placed in prime time and allow simple presentations whose influence can be accumulated by repetition.

The difficulty of communicating to anyone but fellow partisans is the major reason for the appeal of the televised campaign debate, vide the Nixon/Kennedy debate in 1960. Since the debate format reduces the incumbent's advantages in name recognition and partisan inclination, it is not to his advantage.[15] The outcome of the 1960 debate for Nixon's campaign has led most incumbents in every office to refuse, delay, or sabotage a debate format in whatever way possible, despite its public popularity and the desire of the television stations to discharge their public service obligations as cheaply and dramatically as possible. For example, Nixon's substantial initial advantage in 1968 reinforced his disinclination to debate, just as Lyndon Johnson had avoided debate in 1964.

The voter the campaign directors are most eager to reach is the uncommitted, relatively nonpartisan voter. He would seem the easiest target for conversion. Since he lacks deep political convictions, he might indeed be persuaded if he allowed himself to be reached. But this voter has little interest in politics and tunes out the mass media effort. This prevents the mass media from being able to mold the uncommitted voter, who is apathetic about politics and political efforts of persuasion.

To reach this voter, indirect means are necessary. It is here that the organizational effort through precinct campaign workers pays off. The worker can gain votes by face-to-face persuasion of people who have avoided the mass media effort. He can also gain votes on the basis of personal ties, without any persuasion or change in attitude on the part of the politically apathetic. A number of studies have estimated that the difference between good and bad precinct work can add up to 5 per cent of the vote.[16] This difference is a strong endorsement of the continuing value of the campaign effort a party organization can provide even in the age of television. No candidate can duplicate such an organization with only his own resources. An indication of the significance of precinct work was provided by John Lindsay's 1965 New York City mayorality campaign, in which his television budget was cut to finance neighborhood store fronts that waged a face-to-face campaign. The measure was highly controversial but much praised and studied after Lindsay's victory.[17]

The remote, apathetic voter can also be reached by communication from the mass media through his contact with people who do pay attention to the media. Since these "influentials" are likely to share status and group affiliation with those to whom they talk, this indirect effect tends to reinforce existing lines of partisan division. Similarly, the apathetic voter may follow the endorsement of a group leader who himself may be much more involved and ideologically committed. Group communication is dominated by the leadership, which has a privileged access to its membership. This "ideology by proxy" renders group endorsements highly sought after and creates group alignments which appear consistent with ideological voting; for example, the ideological labor union leader who is supported by nonideological union members.[18]

No single campaign strategy is enough for a candidate. He must mix his appeals to a mixture of audiences. This is not a matter of dishonesty, although it may appear so to skeptical observers and certainly helps to create the popular suspicion of campaigning typified by the Mencken quotation. The mixture is demanded by the variation in attention and interest among the voters. Some reference to ideology and/or partisan concerns is needed to motivate the faithful to strong campaign efforts, but this group is too small and committed for exclusive focus. The large share of the electorate (45%) concerned with group benefits requires a large measure of bread-and-butter politics, pointing to specific benefits and programs in each target group, and promising a little bit to everyone regardless of consistency, feasibility, or financial possibility. The category influenced by the nature of the times requires references to the present state of prosperity or lack thereof, or to the undesirable moral climate, or crime in the streets. For those for whom issues are negligible influences, candidate personality and organization efforts are necessary. Above all, the varied and low levels of political information in the audience require that appeals be always explicit and unsubtle.

The length of campaigns is frequently criticized, along with their lack of intellectual stimulation. Yet these characteristics merely follow from the problems suggested above, especially low levels of information, issue conceptualization, and interest. The difficulty of activating one's own supporters and of communicating to the marginal voter requires the long, noisy campaign referred to by Mencken.[19] In fact, a more accurate image of American political campaigning might be "Two blindfolded men sparring before a dozing audience." This too could be something of an exaggeration, but it captures the uncertainty of campaigners and the limited interest and cues provided by the electorate.

Legislative Campaigns and Elections

The legislative campaigner operates in a more secluded environment than candidates for executive positions, especially the chief executives: President, governor, or mayor. There the general focus is on ticket leaders who are usually executives (except for Senators in off-year elections).

For Congressmen and state legislators the campaign is a regularly scheduled event whose chief requirement is that they advertise themselves. The campaign is much less likely to be issue-oriented, because legislators usually cannot make sufficient public impression to generate an issue debate. Therefore, campaigning is not likely of itself to create policy commitments.[20]

The low level of public interest in legislators is shown by the following 1958 poll. Only 47 per cent of the respondents knew which party controlled Congress. When asked about the candidate for Congress in their district, they gave the following replies (Table VIII). Forty-nine per cent of those polled knew something about the incumbent, as compared to 29 per cent for his opponent. This edge biases the electorate in favor of the incumbent and is a significant advantage in the electorate, where recognition of a name may exist without any substantive knowledge to back it.[21]

TABLE VIII

PERCEPTION OF CONGRESSIONAL CANDIDATES*

	%
Knew nothing about either candidate	46
Knew something about both candidates	24
Knew something about incumbent only	25
Knew something about opponent only	5

* SOURCE: Warren Miller and Donald Stokes, "Constituency Influences in Congress," *American Political Science Review,* LVII (March 1963), pp. 53–4.

The low level of knowledge generally forces the legislators into engaging in a perpetual campaign to enhance name recognition and into making broad rather than clearly focused appeals. The emphasis is on creating a favorable image: to appear knowledgeable and trustworthy. Issues are discussed as part of the effort to create this image rather than for their own political value, though the urban Congressman is more likely to make use of formal organization, extensive planning, and more money in his campaign, because they are more readily available to him.[22]

A Congressman generally runs an independent campaign, because the boundaries of a Congressional district frequently do not coincide with those of other electoral districts. The district may divide a city or county or run over a number of counties; rarely is there a single party organization responsible for his nomination. The Congressman gains his nomination from a number of uncoordinated party units or independently of them. Once elected, he can create a personal organization in his district which no one has the inclination or resources to match within those particular boundaries. The separation of Congressional nominations from party organization frees most Congressmen from local organization control, except in the few cities where the traditional organization persists.[23] Usually the Congressman can play off the various units against each other and satisfy their patronage requests without major concessions of autonomy or public policy. The reverse side is the negligible influence Congressmen have on party organization, especially notable in the case of the national convention. For example, Sam Rayburn's power as Speaker of the House meant little when he was trying to get Lyndon Johnson nominated for President in 1960. Powerful figures in the House of Representatives have fared poorly as potential Presidential nominees.[24]

State legislators are more closely linked to party organization, because their districts are smaller and more closely aligned with organizational boundaries such as counties. Furthermore, since state legislatures often have substantial control of local government, the state legislator is often a part of the local leadership.

An important influence on legislative campaigns is the infrequency of closely competitive districts. Less than a quarter of the Congressional seats are closely competitive, as we saw earlier. Even in the highly one-party (60%+) districts, nomination contests are infrequent. Only one-half have nomination contests and only one-quarter result in elections won by less than 2 to 1. Only 4 per cent of Congressmen in the 1944–50 period were defeated for renomination, and very few outside the South where the rate was higher. When there is no incumbent, close fights for the nomination are quite common. In one-party states, the tradition of internal contests leads to a higher degree of nomination competition in safe districts, as again in the South.[25]

The average turnover of Congressmen in general elections from 1954 to 1960 was 6.5 per cent and only 0.5 per cent in the South, mostly in races where the incumbent was not running. The decline in the number of competitive districts also contributes to low turnover. Even in states competitive on the statewide level, the polarization of partisan voting support, and residence patterned by socioeconomic status, reduces competition in the socially more homogeneous districts.[26] Patterns in state legislative elections are similar, with the important exception of frequent voluntary retirements, which enhance the number of seats being contested without incumbents.[27]

The relatively low political mortality rates of legislators does not lull them into tranquility, however. Defeat is always possible, and opportunities occur at the very short intervals provided by the typical two-year term of office. The threat of defeat is made more ambiguous and thereby more challenging by its twofold character. The legislator is in "double jeopardy" because he faces two elections, the general election and the primary, which have two different electorates. He must be sensitive to two different constituencies, one in which the partisan core is highly relevant and another in which the marginal voter is significant. The smaller electorate of the primary can be manipulated more easily than the more diverse and partisanly structured general electorate. A well-financed opponent with a small interest group base is a much greater threat in a primary. The Congressman is therefore very anxious about those who might be able and motivated to launch such a campaign. Particular interest groups will be far more aware of the Congressman's record on matters that concern them than will the general public.

For the state legislator, the "double jeopardy" problem is equally severe, if not more so. He is even less well known to the electorate and his legislative actions are even more obscure. His need to defer to active elements in the constituency is all the greater since they are so few.

Much of the preceding discussion of congressional campaigns, nominations, and elections would give Congressmen cause to say that they arrived in office on their own efforts with little relation to the President or Presidential campaigns. This would seem to be emphasized by the unfocused character of off-year elections.[28] Generally, the out party gains seats, often misinterpreted as a loss of Presidential popularity. What actually happens, however, is a return to more normal divisions of party strength. Presidential elections promote high turnouts of marginal voters, who heavily support the winning party and carry its candidates to victory in marginal districts. Without the Presidential stimulus, turnout drops in the off-year elections and the vote more nearly reflects the balance between strong identifiers for the two parties. Typically, marginal Democratic districts carried in a Republican landslide return to the Democrats, and Republicans similarly bounce back from Democratic Presidential victories.[29]

The Congressmen in these marginal districts are more dependent on the Presidential results and the fortunes of the party label than on their own efforts, since they are relatively unknown and have short tenure. Their dependence on Presidential coattails is reflected in their high voting rate in favor of Presidential programs.[30] For example, the 48 Democrats elected in normally Republican seats in the 1964 Democratic landslide were among the staunchest supporters of the Great Society. In fact, by contributing to this shift of seats from conservative Republicans to liberal Democrats, Barry Goldwater helped to make the Great Society programs possible. Also, the growing Presidential and national committee participation in off-year elections may increase the relevance of Presidential campaign-type issues and appeals. This will at least modestly increase the relation between off-year and Presidential year Congressional elections.[31]

What is the net impact on the Congressman of his campaign activity and the electoral results? One clue is provided by the sensitivity of the Congressman to his constituency. There is considerable agreement between a Congressman's perception of his constituency's views and his voting record, especially on matters close to the constituency's experience, such as civil rights.[32] On matters more remote from the constituents, such as foreign affairs, their perceived attitudes are still influential but not as controlling. However, a Congressman's perception of his constituency's views does not necessarily match its actual views. The perception is filtered through the Congressman's own bias and through the part of the constituency most likely to support him and communicate with him. Both weigh the perception toward the Congressman's existing views. The effective constituency for a Congressman is the sector of it most likely to agree with him. His contact with diehard opponents is rare and unlikely to be weighed as strongly as the frequent contacts of his strongest supporters, who most resemble him.[33]

The Congressman is likely to exaggerate both the agreement and attention he receives from his constituency. One analyst of winners and losers in political campaigns noted a combined congratulation/rationalization effect. The winner sees the result as personal approval of his characteristics and viewpoints. The loser displaces the meaning of the election result as a product of impersonal and uncontrollable factors such as party advantage or lack of funds. In this way, it seems wise to the winner to follow his campaign pledges because he attributes electoral support to them. Because he presumes an attentive audience, he sees political hazards in actions against which interested voters in his constituency might react. He engages in anticipatory responses even though the voters in fact might not react through sheer inattention. By exaggerating the agreement, attention, and personal approval of his constituency, the Congressman can be and very often is highly responsive to it even though the electoral hazards might appear modest. This responsiveness is also heightened by the high degree of uncertainty and instability in the Congressman's primary election constituency, which encourages excessive caution. The emphasis is placed on precautions designed to avoid the necessity of a prolonged primary campaign.[34]

Presidential Nominations

The national nominating process of American democracy operates within the existing limits by accommodating the decentralization of national politics. Thus it attempts to combine unification and conciliation of diverse populations and multiple party factions with the circulation and renewal of party leadership and candidate recruitment. The flexibility and pragmatism of these nomination patterns allows for an effective democratic choice between competitive party leaderships. Some have argued that the national nominating convention should be an object of pride as one of America's most successful innovations in political institutions.[35]

However, events in 1968 apparently sharpened an already existing hostility to this process. Over three-fourths of those polled in September 1968 would have preferred to replace the convention with a single nationwide Presidential primary.[36] This reaction followed closely on the heels of the disastrous Democratic Convention in Chicago, and may subside somewhat in time. Nevertheless, criticism of the convention system has always been common and it does represent substantial issues for democratic government and a desirable political party performance. A close analysis of the Presidential nomination process and of the 1968 Republican and Democratic conventions is needed for a better understanding of these issues.

Two linked themes dominate the national convention: consensus building and campaign preparation.[37] A successful convention for campaign purposes is one which unites and motivates the many elements of the party. There is no means by which partisans can be made to work together; they must be induced to cooperate voluntarily. Even putting the national nominee on the state ballot is a state choice. The national party rests on the free choices of many individuals. This necessary consensus is nurtured by face-to-face encounters and partisan speeches, by collaboration on the party platform, by the coalition building necessary to a majority choice, and by participation in the deliberations over the Vice Presidential nominee. If a convention fails to achieve this consensus, it is a failure, as were both the 1968 Democratic Convention and the 1964 Republican Convention.

Building consensus is aided by the fact that the nomination is open to a variety of influences. The party leadership has a considerable influence on delegate selection and state delegate deliberations. Party rank and file can participate through the preferential primaries. The general electorate is influential through public opinion polls. When the national convention system is working at its best, a broad consensus and enthusiasm develops within the party and its usual supporters to bring about a representative choice.

Running for the presidency entails a complex steeple-chase route to the nomination, via preferential primaries, party organization contacts, and the public opinion polls. It is increasingly unlikely that any one of these elements will alone suffice.

The preferential primaries, especially those in New Hampshire, Wisconsin, and California, play a disproportionate role in the selection process. This is true despite their shortcomings. They are costly and hazardous to the contenders; a candidacy can be destroyed by a single defeat under some circumstances. The opportunities in primaries are often limited by favorite-son candidates and complex rules governing participation. These barriers stem from state organization hostility to the internal struggles a Presidential primary competition can create. The primaries themselves may be unrepresentative of party opinion and needs, because of biases in turnout and the fact that they are not often held in the major states of the Electoral College. The actual vote is often just a popularity poll, with delegates selected separately. Only a minority of delegate votes are gained directly through these Presidential preference primaries.[38]

Nevertheless, the dozen or so preference primaries are a major factor in the nomination outcome. A string of victories can provide impetus toward a bandwagon choice before the convention begins. The task of the party is simplified by eliminating some candidates along the way and the discretion available to the party leaders is reduced to the degree that conclusive patterns develop in the primaries. Candidates have an opportunity to demonstrate their political skills and popular appeal before a variety of audiences. By particular victories, a candidate can demonstrate a basic strength or overcome an apparent weakness. For example, the 1960 West Virginia Democratic Primary was necessary to John F. Kennedy to show that a Catholic could win Protestant Democratic support. Primary victories are necessary for a candidate toward whom the party organization leaders are unsympathetic, the atypical candidate such as Eisenhower or Kennedy. The outsider has to force himself on the organization by reducing its discretion and defeating alternative candidates.[39]

The campaign of Senator Eugene McCarthy for the 1968 Democratic nomination shows how the complexity of the preferential primary route can be used by the outsider. Starting as an unknown to the general public, his unexpected degree of success in New Hampshire gave him the resources and momentum to gain the decisive edge in the Wisconsin primary that hastened President Johnson's withdrawl and contributed to the establishment of the Paris peace talks on Vietnam. The Oregon primary provided him with a second chance after losses to Senator Robert Kennedy in Indiana and Nebraska. Without the chain of individual primaries, McCarthy could not have established himself as a significant Presidential candidate against the persistent skepticism of the mass media reporters and party professionals. In a single nationwide primary he would have lacked the resources and public exposure to contest President Johnson or Vice President Humphrey's nomination. He would not have been able to convince the alienated and fence-sitters that the administration could be beaten, nor the professionals that Vietnam had already divided the party.

On the other hand the classic outsider, Governor Nelson Rockefeller of New York, failed even to attempt the primary route in 1968. The fact that his advisers feared failure in the primaries demonstrated the complete hopelessness of his Presidential ambitions.

In order to work through party organization leaders, a candidate must lobby amid the diffuse party structure, very often with the convention delegates themselves. Since very few state party bosses exist any more, the effort must involve a large number of factional leaders and a considerable acquaintance with the labyrinths of local politics. Here the insider has the best opportunity. Goldwater's wide contacts as senate Campaign committee chairman were quite helpful in this respect. Similarly, Humphrey's long years on the hustings had established for him wide organization leadership sympathy by 1968.[40]

Party organization leaders and convention delegates are inclined to hold off decisions until a likely winner emerges, hence the popularity of favorite-son candidacies. Local factional fights may control alignments, and a concern about the possible impact of the Presidential choice on the success of the local ticket may weigh heavily in the choices made by delegates chosen out of local party organizations. But it should be remembered that the delegates are also concerned citizens who wish to select the best man by their standards. The ambiguity and confusion within this process of choice make the state delegation crucial to information and decision among the heterogeneous and fragmented delegates. Its caucuses and officers provide for a more orderly exchange of information and views on the convention and the candidates than are available elsewhere in the very hectic proceedings of the national convention.[41]

Public opinion polls also impose an important constraint on the choices possible. Poll standings reflect which candidates are sufficiently well known (prominent) to be available for nomination. The unknown cannot be built up quickly enough to provide positive campaign appeal to the electorate. Public opinion polls may not directly influence delegate preferences, but they do strongly influence their perception of who might be a likely winner. And being a winner is a considerable argument to those concerned about the consequences for a successful local campaign. Also, it becomes harder to select someone other than the public favorite if a clear choice exists.

Many feel that in 1968 the polls and public preferences were disregarded. However, the leads in the polls which McCarthy held over Humphrey and Rockefeller held over Nixon among the general electorate were slight and unstable. Moreover, both the eventual nominees were favored by their fellow partisans, whereas both Rockefeller and McCarthy were stronger outside their own party than inside it.[42] Even if one interprets the Democratic primary results as due solely to rejection of the Johnson Administration—and not to any personality impact—the assassination of Robert Kennedy and the withdrawal of President Johnson changed the context of the choice. The weaker of the two anti-Johnson candidates had to defeat someone other than Johnson in the convention itself.

Despite the 1968 results, the older inside strategies based on negotiation among state leaders and dominance of the choice by party organization have been limited by the outside strategies based on Presidential preference primaries and mass media campaigns to build public opinion poll standings provided a decided preference is established.[43] So a mixture of routes to the nomination becomes increasingly necessary. Perhaps the 1960 Kennedy and 1964 Goldwater campaigns best represent the present and future situations. Campaigns must necessarily begin four years in advance. Prominence must be built up by means of published collections of speeches, campaign biographies, overseas trips, and magazine articles. Contacts and coordinators must be developed in every state to influence the party organization. Volunteer organizations must be created to conduct the primary campaign and influence delegate choice in the many areas where party organization is slack. The volunteer organizations also provide good public relations, by reducing the visibility of organization support and emphasizing the popular ground swell for one's candidate. When well laid in advance, these efforts can foreclose the convention result in advance, as in the examples of John Kennedy and Barry Goldwater. Robert Kennedy was following the same strategy before his death with considerable success and might well have won the nomination.

Removal of the two-thirds requirement for nomination by the Democrats in 1936 and, more important, the growing legitimacy of public opinion polls, have largely negated the relevance of dark-horse candidacies. Creating a deadlocked convention is far more difficult now and disastrous if it occurs. The unknown candidate is too great a handicap in the Presidential election where candidate appeal is a large component in the choice.

The sources from which Presidential candidates emerge are also changing. Formerly, governors were favored by their control of state convention delegations and their lack of involvment on controversial national issues; but their advantages have diminished as a result of the current growing pains of state government, and the weakening of state party organization and of their control over convention delegations. Conversely, Senators can use their longer terms of office to select a desirable public image and blunt the effect of controversial choices. More important, Senators can identify themselves with foreign policy expertise, a major and growing criterion in voter choice for the Presidency. Vice Presidents are coming into the limelight because their national, foreign policy, and party roles have all been strengthened by the Twenty-second Amendment limiting Presidential tenure to two elected terms. Prominence can now come easily to that formerly most obscure of American officials.[44]

A relevant problem for Presidential contenders is the growing expense of national campaigns, involving preference primaries and the mass media. The primaries cannot be ignored and their expense virtually eliminates all but very rich men from effective competition, for example, Humphrey in 1960. Only a man with considerable advantages in prominence can tap major campaign funds without relying on personal wealth, although the McCarthy campaign may provide contrary evidence. Here the significance of the growing stature of the vice presidency is manifest as a place from which a man of more moderate means can receive the public exposure necessary for the presidency: witness the 1960 and 1968 campaigns of Richard Nixon, and the 1968 campaign of Hubert Humphrey.

The selection of the Presidential and Vice Presidential

nominees is the most conspicuous act of the national party convention, but it is not the only important activity performed there. Equally important is the process of creating the party cohesion necessary to conduct a national campaign. In acting as a governing body and campaign rally and in adopting a party platform, the national convention exceeds the scope of a national Presidential primary.

The national convention is the principal formal organization achieved by the national party. For four or five days each four years, the diverse elements of each party are physically together and acting. The national convention not only makes rules for its own proceedings (largely concerning the nomination struggles) but also regulates the minimal continuing national organization, the national committee. Together these two units exercise the little formal authority available to the national party.[45]

One of the most important consequences of the McCarthy campaign was the 1968 rule changes made at the Democratic Convention. Although most will not take effect until 1972, the abolition of the binding unit rule in selection of delegates and their voting, the enforcement of the requirement for delegations representative of state party support, and the limitation of centralized and/or early selection of delegates will all enhance the democratic character of future Democratic conventions and have dealt with serious flaws in the existing selection process in a number of states, especially but not exclusively in the South.[46] Each of these rule changes undercuts the capacity of established party leaders to shut out new party activists and their candidates. The Democratic example will probably force similar adjustments of the Republican rules to avoid invidious comparisons.

The national convention is significant as the campaign rally which opens the drive for the presidency. The rhetoric of this occasion provides the initial campaign involvment and motivation for the party rank and file. It is the major opportunity to build a sense of purpose among the diverse elements of the party. A successful convention can create a fighting spirit and a "we" feeling among fellow partisans.[47] In this respect, the 1968 Democratic Convention managed to be a total failure.

As a campaign rally, the convention has the considerable advantage over other campaign efforts of a bi-partisan television audience, by far the largest single audience of the entire campaign. This fact has led to a streamlining of the "show" and has somewhat reduced its emotive value for the convention delegates themselves.[48] Indeed, the delegates have been reduced to watching television to find out what is going on. The number of convention delegates, especially the Democrats, has grown far too large for an effective deliberative body. The democratic value of extensive representation should perhaps be balanced by revising convention procedures so as to permit more effective delegate participation. The control over floor microphones by the convention leadership in Chicago certainly left much to be desired.

Television coverage of national conventions has clearly gotten out of hand. The size of convention halls and the poor acoustics for the delegates themselves are closely related to the requirements of television coverage. The inflation and repetition of rumors give floor reporters a chance to create artificial drama and disrupt the efforts of delegates to deliberate. The "entertainment" requirement rewards a coverage of conflict and division that is reinforced by publicity. Thus, the interests of the networks are directly antagonistic to the party leadership's need to build up consensus and harmony, and to the delegates' desire to participate. The task of revising traditional convention practices and television coverage of the convention needs more thoughtful attention than it has received to date.

The intention to build up national party identity and cohesion also lies behind the effort of writing a party platform. Party platforms are often treated with scorn and regarded as hopelessly vague and meaningless; yet, every four years, a great number of busy, practical men devote considerable effort to their construction. Moreover, very bitter battles over wording frequently occur, witness the Vietnam plank at the 1968 Democratic Convention. Something of value must be involved to arouse such effort and passion.

The party platform can provide recognition of allied interest groups, and diverse party factions can point to planks of the party platform which recognize their individual status.[49] By these means the party coalition is strengthened and factions that fail to nominate their Presidential candidate still achieve a measure of success. It is for this reason that the platform comes before the nomination. The platform belongs to the party, not to the candidate. The various factions are being rewarded and deferred to, because the decision is still in doubt and the party as a whole is involved and committed to it. If the platform were to be adopted after the candidate had been selected, it would attract less interest and could not be used so easily for consensus building, which would reduce its value. Moreover, the successful candidate would be more responsible for it, thereby reducing his campaigning and governing discretion.

But the platform is a campaign document as well as a means to internal party cohesion. And as a campaign aid it reflects the care of the drafting process. Vagueness occurs when voters are unclear, uninterested, or divided. Majority positions are endorsed and long-standing divisions of party support reflected in platform differences. Pledges are specific when a specific target group exists. Each party has identifiable and stable attributes in platform composition. Platforms provide meaningful indications of the party's intentions, since they typically represent a partisan consensus reached in the drafting process.[50]

The scope of a national Presidential primary would be more limited than that of a national convention because the primary is only concerned with the Presidential nomination. Furthermore, popular assumptions about the democratic nature of national Presidential nominating primaries overlook several factors which contrast unfavorably with the convention system.[51] For example, the biases in primary turnouts, the tremendous expense of a national primary campaign, and the high likelihood of plurality victories would all work to the detriment of the outsider, the candidate supposedly handicapped by the present system. All the disadvantages of state primaries would be compounded for the maverick candidate because of the magnitude of the resources needed to wage a campaign in fifty states at once. Moreover, no means of gaining party cohesion would be available without the impact of the convention as a cooperative venture, a campaign rally, and a place to emphasize partisan agreement on a party platform. Instead, Presidential candidates would have to exploit divisions within the party and concerns of the party faithful at the expense of the marginal voters who will decide the general election outcome. The concurrent selection of the Vice Presidential nominee could create ill-assorted tickets and give rise to Vice Presidents who could not be trusted or prepared by the President for the possibility of succession.

The Presidential nominating system in the United States is unique for a variety of reasons, which is highly desirable because the presidency requires unique attributes; its occupant is both head of state and head of government, at once the symbol of unity and leader of political conflict. There is no accustomed route to power: educational background, legislative experience, party organization work, or positions held. Experience in public service and adherence to party doctrine, the keystones of the parliamentary line of leadership recruitment, are here neglected. The emphasis can be instead on reaching beyond the regulars to a variety of leadership sources, on the possession of popular appeal, and on diverse pluralistic political skills. Above all, the selection process is flexible, capable of varying to meet new demands, although not necessarily always succeeding.

Presidential Election Campaigns

Most of the previous comments on campaigning apply also to Presidential campaigns. The scale, intensity, and confusion is magnified but the problems of finance planning, and information feedback are similar. A Presidential candidate is relatively better off in his efforts to acquire the necessary resources and attention, but he can always use more time, more money, more staff, and more mass media exposure than he will ever have.

In the early phase of the campaign he needs time to organize his campaign and complete the process of uniting the party behind him. The late date of the 1968 Democratic Convention (which had been scheduled to coincide with President Johnson's birthday at a time when he had been expected to be his party's candidate) denied Hubert Humphrey the usual month or so before Labor Day. By mid-October, his campaign organization had hardly reached the typical late-August level of readiness.

The later phases of a Presidential campaign usually concentrate on activating the party workers and reinforcing already favorable political attitudes and partisanship; in addition, efforts are made to neutralize, if not convert, potential opposition. Nixon in 1968, for example, used relatively nonpartisan appeals to prevent pro-Democratic mobilization. His own partisans had already been reconciled by skillful handling before the convention and by their own great eagerness for victory. The major issues, Vietnam and "law 'n' order" had only to be mentioned to activate and reinforce anti-administration votes, while vague, bland proposals kept these votes together.

Humphrey was unable to parry this tactic because the Chicago convention had completed the estrangement of a large proportion of the most effective party workers. Not only was the early phase of the campaign destroyed, but the lack of enthusiasm among those McCarthy supporters who finally voted for Humphrey limited the amount of precinct work done on his behalf, resulting in secondary losses among voters not contacted or mobilized. In such a close election, the fact that the Republicans had an edge of three to two in frequency of door-to-door campaigning benefitted them substantially in 1968.[52]

The traditional Democratic appeals to the working class were less effective in 1968 because George Wallace mobilized anxiety and fear about race-related issues. However, the dropoff in Wallace support in late October, combined with the activation of Democratic inclinations plus the halt in American bombing of North Vietnam enabled Humphrey to close the gap. McCarthy supporters were slow in responding to partisan and "the lesser of three evils" appeals, which meant that there was a strong political inducement for President Johnson's last-minute cessation of the bombing.

Presidential campaigns in other years have differed from those in 1968 as the particular events and issues varied, but it is clear that the campaign itself has been increasingly nationalized, responding less to local issues and characteristics. Television coverage has reduced the feasibility of special speeches to specific audiences; it has also served to unify the concern of voters over the entire country. For example, the citizens of a small town in Kansas were highly concerned about urban riots and hippies in 1968, even though they had no direct experience of either.[53] The Chicago demonstrations provoked reactions and judgments from voters throughout the nation. As a result, the task of balancing appeals and conducting a coherent Presidential campaign has become more complex.

Summary

Political campaigns can serve four functions of great value to the American society: they can test the candidates, involve the public in formulating public policy, mediate public policy conflict, and legitimize the resulting governmental decisions. Each of these functions relies heavily on the existence of the political party mechanism as a primary means to their fulfillment.

Campaigns can test the candidate's skills for democratic politics: his ability to work with other political actors, to grasp the political "facts of life," and to make the best use of available resources. Campaigns test his capacity to attract able men to his service and use their advice intelligently, which is necessary for any effective public official. Furthermore, campaigns test a candidate's capacity to build a consensus for his programs, not to mention his personal qualities under stress.[54] The testing is not complete, of course.

The length and strenuousness of the campaign serve to involve the public, inform it on public issues, and increase its active participation in politics.[55] The need for an active, responsible citizenry coincides with the party organizations' need for recruits. Government is made more meaningful and relevant by campaign appeals and efforts, which inform and sensitize voters.

In organizing agreement and disagreement on public affairs, the campaigns and the political parties contribute to the expression and mediation of conflict. Of course, under some circumstances they sharpen conflict, but they also give it an opportunity to effect the political process. In its conclusion (the election itself), the campaign provides an alternative to violence as a means of registering grievances, and so helps to achieve the peaceful transition of governmental authority.

The campaign, the policy discussion, party programs, and candidate pledges all sanction the acts of public officials after election. However tenuous the mandate theory may be in terms of public issue awareness and concern, the fact remains that both officials and the public permit and perceive policy conclusions to be drawn from election results. In a broader sense, the public involvment in and discussion of policy choices in a campaign creates a psychological link to the subsequent choices which eases the acceptance of new policy, even by those opposed to it. Without this cushion of acceptance based on a presumably fair opportunity to participate and influence the popular choice, democratic government could not retain the confidence of its citizens needed for effective decisions.[56]

If one looks beyond the noise and exaggeration of the campaign, its contribution to democratic government is considerable. Of course, the benefits do depend on the quality and context of the campaign. A landslide election is not very revealing or demanding of the victor, as many who voted for Lyndon Johnson in 1964 discovered, and campaigns based on fear and hate reduce the legitimacy of whoever is elected, by reducing confidence among groups in the society and toward public officials. Bland programs do nothing to secure citizen participation and support after the election.

Nevertheless, Presidential elections can be decisive influences on political parties by creating, reinforcing or disrupting partisan coalitions. In so doing, they affect the policy mixture common to a successful party. The guidelines of elections are crude but they do furnish indications of public policy. Elections choose the officials who will choose public policy, and the different compositions of the two parties mean different probabilities for individual public policy alternatives. Thus, although the elections are ambiguous and grant great discretion and initiative to public officials, they influence the directions in which that discretion is likely to be exercised. In 1932, the electorate did not call for the New Deal, but it did vote for the candidate more likely to innovate and endorsed those innovations in the 1936 landslide.

What meaning can be assigned to elections per se? What we know of voting behavior suggests that most commentators overinterpret the results. Operating from highly rationalistic and abstract conceptions of politics, they are quite likely to attribute their own concerns and ideals to the voter. We have to reconcile the outcomes of elections with the low level of sophistication and interest that is characteristic of the average voter, since most advocates of democratic theory operate on individualistic assumptions. For them, the whole must equal the sum of its parts—if the average voter falls short of their standard, the outcome of elections are considered to be equally irrational and ill-formed. They question whether intelligent collective decisions are possible without a preponderance of individually intelligent decisions.

Such analysis is at fault in the seemingly plausible assumption that the whole is equal simply to the sum of its parts, that good voters mean good elections which mean good government. In fact, the whole is *greater* than the sum of its parts; the election as a collective decision is of a different character to individual voter decisions. By evaluating three different models of voter—philosophic, citizen, manipulated subject, and private partisan[57]—we can demonstrate this.

Clearly, the average voter does not fit the "philosophic citizen" model (rational, concerned, and informed) that Progressives, Nonpartisans, and Party Government advocates assume and/or require. However, it is not clear that this is completely unfortunate, since a moderate amount of citizen apathy may actually be desirable. A high proportion of ideologues and overintense concern could reduce the tolerance of inconsistent choices which in fact enables leaders to satisfy the multiple and contradictory demands of a heterogeneous society and economy. A more sharply defined public opinion and high intensity of citizen involvement would mean higher expectations and demands of government, perhaps more than could be satisfied. The governmental system might thus become unworkable, losing its legitimacy and public support.[58] Against this, it must be stressed that apathy is not distributed equally throughout the electorate. When combined with either subtle or crude discrimination, it may further reduce the political effectiveness of those who are already disadvantaged.[59] Voter apathy is probably most beneficial to the white middle class which moralizes about it.

In contrast, many fear that the voter is so poorly informed that he can be easily manipulated and popular control of government reduced to a sham; this is the theory of the "manipulated subject." The power of the mass media could possibly lead to the domination of government by public relations experts—men who are trained in creating images, fears, and desires (Eugene Burdick's *The 480* and *The Ninth Wave* are the popularizations of this model[60]). In actual fact, however, indifference to politics probably insulates the uninformed from media persuasion. Their identification with their party stabilizes voting behavior against short-term manipulation, and the inheritance of political attitudes and partisan affiliations through group memberships ties them to attitudes consistent with the continuing interests of those groups.

Much more impressive is the evidence for the third model, the "private partisan." The voter reacts when his own interests are threatened—two-thirds of American voters for the presidency fall into the "group benefits" and "nature of times" categories of issue conceptualization. Partisan identification may not be rationally formed, but the alignment is usually consistent with rational self-interest. The voter might not see all the implications of the political choices to be made, but he has a good eye for those that are most immediately relevant to him. He may be shortsighted and relatively narrow in his concerns, and therefore private in his partisanship, but he is not irrational in his choices.[61]

Finally, too much concern with the vagaries of voters may mislead one in evaluating elections. After all, roughly a fifth of the electorate shifts its choice from one election to another and the alignments usually result in consistency between policy preferences and voting choice.[62] Not all policy preferences can be satisfied in a single party, because diverse majorities exist on each issue. No single dividing line could organize all policy debate in the complex, pluralistic American society. Parties are loosely coordinated in their programmatic appeals and bases of support. Their decentralization reduces their capacity to carry out an election mandate, but this is part of the same process which limits the likelihood of a single, clear-cut mandate being expressed by the voters. Stronger mandates from election results would distort the social, economic, and political reality in the United States.

American political parties provide a means for popular consultation that parallels this diversity without downgrading majority rule as much as the Status-Quo prototype suggests. Elections are not intended primarily to ensure desirable positive government action, but rather as a means of making government *responsible*. As the "private partisan" model indicates, elections are used to protect immediate interests and to control officials by penalizing past actions. An example of this is the recent expansion of Black voting in the South, which has had more influence in reducing police brutality and capital punishment than in advancing school desegregation, where immediate white interests are involved.[63] This emphasis on responsibility and past action, rather than a positive program, illustrates how the "private partisan" model of the voter, the interpretation of elections as protective devices for the voter, and the Responsible Parties prototype of political parties are all consistent with one another.

VI. the pervasiveness of party in government

THE POLITICAL PARTY influences government, not because of party discipline or organization, but because of the thoroughgoing way in which parties have pervaded all government levels and the manner in which they bias recruitment to government office. Partisan differences manifest themselves without compulsion and often without a high degree of self-consciousness on the part of government officials. This is possible because political parties filter, reinforce, and organize the relevant attitudes and sustain policy differences, without individuals explicitly having to decide to follow a party line.

The most demanding and necessary test of the relevance of political parties is their role in government itself—the acts of public officials and the making of public policy. The range of partisan activity within government is an important measure of the impact of the partisanship found in voting behavior, campaigning, and elections. This chapter stresses the analysis of partisanship in legislative activity. It is through legislating that the principal guidelines for public policy are fashioned and the content of party programs most directly expressed. The advantages of a partisan organization of legislatures are offset by constituency pressures and the committee system. Nevertheless, the party leadership has considerable assets which permit and encourage partisan choices, especially its relationship to the chief executive, and the recruitment of individual legislators. The outcome is a legislative policy which is often more partisan than is usually recognized. Administrative and judicial personnel are also sometimes partisan as a consequence of their recruitment. What emerges from this analysis is the pervasiveness and fundamental unity of partisan behavior and influence in American politics.

Partisan Organization of Legislatures

Political parties are fundamental to the organization of legislatures in the United States. Partisanship determines the selection of the presiding officer and general responsibility for conducting the business of the legislative body in Congress, all but one state legislature, and a majority of city councils in the larger cities.[1] The influence attached to presiding over and conducting legislative activity provides the basis of the governmental role of political parties. A state party chairman was once asked why he helped to elect a state representative of dubious character, low party regularity, and personal enmity toward the chairman. He replied that while most of this legislator's votes in a session might be cast against the party, "the first vote is ours."

The organization of the United States Congress is the best-known demonstration of the party role in legislative organization. In the House of Representatives, the nominee of the majority party is selected Speaker of the House, and the minority nominee is minority leader and will become Speaker if his party gains a majority of seats. On this vote, every party member votes for his party's nominee. Party line voting is absolute on this question, even if not on any other issue in the session. Party division also controls the division of memberships on committees, with the majority party holding the chairmanship and a share of committee seats proportionate to its share of the House seats.

The leadership of the majority party is held by the Speaker and the House Majority Leader, both nominated by party caucus in what is usually a simple reconfirmation of the previous session's choices. The Speaker as presiding officer is primarily responsible for control over agenda, through his power to recognize speakers in debate, and his relationship with the Rules Committee and committee chairman. Once legislative business comes out of committee, its flow is greatly influenced by his discretionary powers. The Majority Leader is primarily responsible for dealing with the rank-and-file members of the legislative party. Through the chief Majority Whip and his assistants, he distributes information on the schedule, counts voting support on various bills, and learns about the attitudes and concerns of individual members. The party leadership exerts influence on the Committee on Committees which makes assignments to committee vacancies.[2] The minority party has a similar leadership, whip, and committee assignment structure, but it must negotiate with the majority leadership to influence the agenda of the House because it lacks direct control over the legislative organization.

In the Senate, the party organization is similar except that the power of the presiding officer, the Vice President, is limited and agenda control is exercised by the Senate Majority Leader. The Senate's smaller size and the power of an individual Senator to hinder proceedings reduce the significance of the formal party organization when compared to the larger, more complex, and necessarily less flexible House of Representatives.

In both Houses, the flow of legislation depends on the priority in recognition given to the majority leader by the presiding officer. Since it is frequently necessary to suspend rules by a two-thirds vote or unanimous consent in order to expedite business, advance consultation and agreements with the minority leader are necessary. By this means, the minority leader has bargaining advantages and therefore influence on the agenda and related behavior. By consulting in advance, the majority and minority leaders can decide such items as the time allocated to debate or the order of consideration of amendments. These matters may help to shape legislative outcomes.[3]

There is considerable variation in the influence of individual party leaders in the same formal positions, especially in the Senate; for example, mild-mannered Mike Mansfield was a far less effective Democratic Senate Majority Leader than the more aggressive Lyndon Johnson.[4] This personal variation reflects the slackness of party organization in Congress, which can take many forms. The Congressional party has a fragile, limited leadership structure.

The variations in state legislatures make it difficult to give anything between the briefest or most detailed descriptions. Many of the same elements described for Congress are present, the partisan presiding officer, majority and minority party leaders, whip organization, partisan committees on committee assignments. Their importance varies widely from one state to another, but certain generalizations are possible. In few states are the committee structures as thoroughly stabilized by seniority traditions as in Congress. Party leaders can often reshape committees from one session to another and ignore seniority claims to a committee chairmanship. On occasion in a few states, the committee chairman or committee majority may not be of the majority party. The limitations on length of session, and the relatively small proportion of experienced members, give the party leadership in state legislatures formidable tactical advantages not available to their national counterparts.[5] As the leading scholar on this subject has said, the state legislators are "organized for strong leadership" and for reasons to be discussed more fully later, this leader is likely to be governor.[6]

Limitations of the Legislative Party

The resources and effectiveness of the legislative party are limited both from outside the legislative body and from within. The constituency weakens the allegiance of the member of party leaders in the legislature and forces his concern outside. Inside the legislature, the committees, reinforced by the seniority system, provide rewards and punishments in rivalry to the party leaders.

The impact of the constituency is twofold. The legislators have two sets of risks in the constituency, those associated with the general election and those associated with the primary. The primary electorate is relatively small and narrow in its concerns. The support of the legislative party leadership in the primary is likely to be negligible, and resented even if available. When a strong constituence interest is at stake, the member is expected to vote against the party, if necessary.[7] This practice is widespread in legislatures and tolerated by party leaders even when the legislative party organization is very strong. In the New York or Connecticut legislatures, it is like getting an "excused absence" from the party line.[8]

The constituency orientation of the legislator is supported by the disruption and decline of party organization. Lacking a stable set of supporters and workers, the legislator cannot aflord to offend any well-organized and intense interest group in his constituency. He must concentrate on the risks and rewards in his own district at the expense of supporting the party. Of course, strong party organization could also reinforce constituency orientation or receptivity to particular interest groups, depending on the leadership and openness of the party organization.

The location of the principal electoral risks for the legislator in this diffuse primary constituency decentralizes the legislative party. The purge attempted by Franklin Roosevelt in 1938 did not fail because of local party organization resistance, but because of the lack of a responsive party organization that the President could use against the incumbent legislators. Where there was a sympathetic local party organization, such as in Representative O'Connor's district in Manhattan, Roosevelt was able to defeat the incumbent.[9] Typically, the personal organization of the legislative incumbent was superior to the necessarily ad hoc organizations used by President Roosevelt. The Hatch Act passed by Congress in 1940 limited the political activities of national government civil servants and limited patronage positions. It was not a silly, spiteful reaction, as sometimes interpreted, but an intelligent countermove to ensure that the President could not act to create more effective local party organization. The patronage lost by Congressmen was less important than denying the opportunity it created for centralization of the legislative party.[10] In states where the governor still has extensive patronage, legislators can be made more amenable to his influence by the potential for purges through local organizations.[11] This is not a common situation, however, and decentralization of the state legislative party is widespread.

While the constituency limits the legislative party from outside the legislature, the committee system limits it within the institution. The committee system of American legislatures plays a very large role in legislative activity, especially in Congress, but also in many state legislatures. Many see this role as all-powerful and speak of "little legislatures." In committees, nearly all minor bills and most details of major legislation are given the bulk of their consideration. The decisions of the legislature, except for major legislation, largely ratify committee decisions. Legislative committees are also the basic mechanism by which administrative performance is supervised and modified, especially in the national government. The committees gain influence through the operation of seniority, an emphasis on routine, and specialization. It is the weakness of these three processes in many state legislatures that leads them to have weaker committee systems.[12]

When seniority practices are fully developed, they provide a powerful barrier to partisan leadership influence. Assignment to committees is based on seniority and length of continuous service in the legislature. Chairmanship of the committee goes to the member of the majority party with the longest continuous service on that particular committee. When seniority always controls committee appointments and status, the member's influence is dependent on successive reelections and on his responsiveness to the committee chairman. A careful attention to his constituency at the expense of party interests is desirable because it ensures his accumulation of seniority. This is true as long as the voters or the local party do not require party regularity, as they usually do in Great Britain.[13]

The emphasis on routine refers to the settled continuing patterns of handling legislation. Bills must be assigned to fixed, standing committees and must undergo the usually elaborate deliberative processes of the committee. The committees control the pace of consideration and can adapt it to their needs. This limits the legislative tactics available to party leaders.

Specialization involves both the committee as a whole and its members individually. Through specialization, the committee and its members become more experienced and knowledgeable about a given subject. The appropriate government agencies and interest groups come to their hearing and deliberations and by developing expertise, both the committee and its members become more influential with other legislators who lack it. The specialist legislator is valuable to other legislators because he also takes electoral risks on his choices. His advice is therefore more meaningful than that of an outside expert, however well informed, who does not face the same risks.[14]

The continuity and specialized knowledge found in the well-developed committee system make its participants very influential in formulating public policy. Few of their decisions are reviewed by the legislature as a whole. The favors they can do for other members mean that the committee has rewards available that compete favorably with any available to the party leaders. The committee system builds a fortress around each specific field of legislation.

The constituency oriented member and the seniority-based committee system are complementary in their indifference to the needs and pressures of the legislative party leadership.

Party Leadership Assets

How can the party leaders exercise influence in such unpromising circumstances? Somewhat surprisingly, the very nature of the resources of the committee system provide the answer. The narrow focus of the committees, their fortress-like aspects, gives them power in one substantive field of legislation at the expense of power elsewhere. The forts are not interlinked but isolated. The committees are in competition to have their output approved by Congress or the state legislature. Also, the timing of consideration of a bill may be crucial to its chances of passage. The legislative system requires communication and coordination.

The committee chairmen cannot band together to provide this coordination because of jealousy for their own prerogatives, and more important, the demanding nature of their committee work. The party leaders, on the other hand, have control of the flow of business, the power to set agenda, and the information system provided by the leadership structure. They are at the center of communications and know the stages at which legislation is in various committees, the number of legislators available to vote, and the probable division of opinion. They know less about any one thing but more about everything. They are the generalists necessary to coordinate the specialists.[15] The party leaders operate the only widespread communication network available in the legislature and calls must be placed with them. They can facilitate "log-rolling" among diverse groupings to work out a bill providing benefits to each and obligating them to the party leaderships for the service performed.[16]

The larger size of the House of Representatives makes the use of formal communication networks more necessary there than in the Senate, where one or a small group of Senators could maintain an informal nonparty communication network to offset partially the leadership's advantages. The size of the House of Representatives also requires more rigid adherence to formal procedures in order to conduct business efficiently. Since the leaders must apply and enforce these complex rules, their discretionary powers are enhanced. In state legislatures, limited sessions and low levels of experience in the membership reinforce the formal powers of party leaders in scheduling.[17]

Supplementing these resources are the discretionary choices left to the leadership where there are gaps in the seniority system. While senior members of the legislature have usually achieved the committee posts they want, the newer members may want transfers to more desirable committees. By putting loyal legislators on the Committee on Committees, the party leadership can reward the applicants who have cast more party line votes, especially when members with equal seniority apply for the same position. The response to party leadership discretion in committee assignment appears to be related to the higher party voting record of junior members of the legislative party.[18] As Speaker of the House Sam Rayburn said, "To get along, go along." This pattern is aided by the small favors the party leadership can give a newer member in terms of recognition, local campaign appearances, and small amount of money from legislative campaign funds which aid in establishing him in his own constituency. Thus, Jesse Unruh diverted campaign donations to enough needy assemblymen candidates to build a major power base and become Speaker of the California State Assembly.[19]

The resources of the majority party leader are shared with the minority party leader because the majority leader needs his cooperation on scheduling. As a result, the minority party leader can reward members of his party, influence committee assignments, and build support for his continued tenure as leader. His power within his party is "shadow" power, a pale derivative of the majority party leadership influence. But he is at a key point in the communication network, possessing valuable information on probable minority party voting alignment and on the progress of various committees through the minority membership.[20] The close link with the majority party leader creates tensions for the minority leader, who must simultaneously oppose and cooperate. If he cooperates too well, he may be deposed by those who want more aggressive leadership, as was the problem of Joseph Martin. If he concentrates on opposition, he may not be able to work the bipartisan arrangements he needs to reward supporters, and he then becomes vulnerable to a challenge by members without reasons for strong loyalty to him, as Charles Halleck found.[21]

Two leadership groups contend for influence over the legislature and its members: the committee system, headed by the seniority leaders and based on control over the substance of legislation; and the party organization leadership, which organizes the flow of legislative business and is based on control of communication and scheduling. At extremes each can stalemate the other, so it is in their mutual interest to bargain and cooperate without open conflicts. Party leaders facilitate passage of legislation in return for committee modifications toward their preferences. The party leaders can communicate to the committee chairmen the probable chances of passage of a bill by polling their membership and shifting the timing and context of its consideration favorably. On the major bills, the party leaders are more likely to exercise the preponderant influence, because they are more willing and able to interest and mobilize the membership for such issues. On minor legislation, passage of committee results is likely to be routine and without challenge.[22] The two leadership groups are thus mutually dependent and interdependent, so that bargaining becomes a primary aspect of the legislative process.

The Chief Executive and the Legislative Party

The communication network of the legislative party leadership is linked to the chief executive. Here too is a relationship of mutual dependence. The chief executive and the legislative party leaders need each other and benefit by cooperation.

In the American system of limited government, chief executives characteristically lack a stable base of political support and assured government authority. They must form ad hoc coalitions on individual issues and rely on persuasion, not coercion, to achieve their objectives. Moreover, chief executives usually lack the time and political resources needed to build their own legislative leadership. Therefore, they have to work with the existing party structure in the legislature to carry out their legislative program. This lack of alternatives enables the legislative party leaders to exact a price for their cooperation.

On the other hand, the legislative party leaders need the chief executive's resources to reward their supporters and enhance their own influence. Their authority in the legislature is needed to bargain with the governor or President and their relationship with the chief executive enables them to maintain their influence in the legislature. If one asks whether they are the legislature's representatives to the executive or vice versa, the best answer is that they "need to be both, to be either."[23]

What are the executive resources which the legislative leaders can use? Patronage and government contracts or facilities are vastly overrated. Most jobs and other government favors are under the control of legislative committees or governmental agencies, which prefer to use them to add to their own support rather than aid the executive. These resources, though presumed by the public to make "arm-twisting" pressure available, actually reduce the net influence of the chief executive rather than adding to it. Only in a few states, mostly Southern, is the gubernatorial patronage sufficient to be a source of strength. In these cases, the governor regularly organizes his own legislative faction and puts through his program on a high-pressure, high-payoff basis, but this is an exceptional and increasingly rare case.[24]

The executive-legislative relationship is based rather on the chief executive's role as the major source of legislative initiative. His budget and legislative program provide the basic coherence for the legislative session. He gives the legislature a guide to the desires of the biggest customer for its output (the executive branch), provides the major issues as the focus of popular and legislative attention, creates a ready-made workload for the committees, gives clues as to where he might exercise his veto, and gives legislators opportunities to tie their pet projects to the coattails of his program.[25]

The chief executive has the initiative in legislation because of the growing demands on government to provide and finance a wide variety of programs. Being the most visible and best-known public official in the state or nation, his acts receive publicity disproportionately greater than that available to legislators. For this reason, he is held responsible for governmental performance and his initiatives define what will be the major issues. He is in the best position to assemble the resources for innovation, because he is best able to gain the public attention and support necessary to influence and coordinate the many veto points produced by a fragmented government structure.

Legislative initiative is difficult hampered by the dispersal of power into the individual committees. Where matters are left to their discretion, the committees can initiate successfully. Because of their detailed legislative activity, often they can more effectively supervise individual government bureaus than the chief executive can.

The minority party cannot respond effectively to the chief executive's initiatives because it lacks the mechanisms to present alternative programs. The seniority leaders on their side resist coordination and the minority legislative party leadership is weaker than its majority counterpart. Moreover, the legislative party is one of many elements of the opposition party. Even if it could be coordinated, the minority party could not command the public coverage that the chief executive can. An illustrative example was the 1967 Presidential State of the Union Message, which carried on all television and radio networks at prime time, followed by a Republican reply a week or so later on a few networks late in the evening. This difference in media treatment was not deliberate discrimination, but a reasonable estimate of relative public interest.

Because of the importance of his legislative initiative, a knowledge of the chief executive's program, priorities, and probable tactics is very valuable information for members of the legislature. This is true regardless of whether or not they favor his desires, because the knowledge can influence their own priorities and tactics. By having the best access to this information, the legislative party leaders can maximize uncertainty when it is a tactical advantage or give members information as part of their attempts to persuasion. They can advise the chief executive on the progress of his legislation, the division of support, and possible means of achieving a majority on the basis of their intralegislative communication network. To facilitate the party leaders' success, the chief executive makes his resources available to them, in order to enhance the effectiveness of the legislative party organization. The flow of information and political resources is two-way; each exercises influence over the other.[26]

Information and the best ways of gathering and using it are crucial ingredients of the influence which sustain the legislative party organization against powerful rivals in the committee system and the constituency. The basis of the party organization's effectiveness is subtle and complex. For this reason, legislative party leadership depends heavily on the personal skills of the occupants of the party offices and the legislative party's influence varies widely at different times.

Supporting Conditions for Legislative Partisanship

The discussion so far has stressed the constituency pressures on the legislator not to support the legislative party. A legislator's constituency does limit his choice in areas where specific interest exists, but the constituency may be indifferent on many issues. For example, the very intensity of involvement of one district in agricultural matters will make a deep concern for mining legislation unlikely. The homogeneous district reduces the legislator's freedom of choice on some matters, but makes others irrelevant to his constituents. Most of the voting decisions he has to take are in this zone of indifference. Therefore, the legislator can seldom be a simple recording agent of constituent choices. One of his frequent worries and complaints is lack of guidance, not excessive pressure.[27] How does the legislator exercise choice in the absence of strong constituency pressures? A number of factors contribute to a partisan pattern: an "effective" constituency, legislative group socialization, partisan recruitment channels, and a shared stake in the party label, all tending to support party loyalty.

Legislators' constituencies are quite varied in composition, but certain consistent differences do appear. Republicans are more likely to be elected from less urban, more middle-class, more older-immigrant-stock, more white, and more Protestant constituencies than Democrats.[28] Constituencies as a group tend to magnify those characteristics which are associated with party voting. Thus, the 60 per cent of the constituency to which a Republican legislator is most likely to respond is composed of those social groups more distinctively Republican and more likely to vote for him. (Even when they share occupations, Republican and Democratic Senators differ markedly. For example, Republican businessmen are likely to be publishing and manufacturing executives, while Democratic businessmen in the Senate are likely to be noncorporate, independent entrepreneurs.[29]) It is from one of those groups that the Republican candidate is most likely to be recruited. These are the people whom he is most likely to know personally and whose opinions will reach and influence him most easily. This nonrepresentative section of his constituency is known as his "effective" constituency.

The effective constituencies of Republican or Democratic legislators as a group are therefore even more similar than the total constituencies they represent. This is especially true in states where party composition is close and sharply polarized along SES lines. Both conditions hold in the more urban and industrialized states. A growing minority party, usually associated with urbanizing and industrializing trends, also contributes to constituency differentiation between the two parties.[30] The consequence of these polarizations is a reduction in the conflict between constituency and party. Since they share social groups and group interests, similar policy choices will satisfy both. Republicans and Democrats can reflect their constituencies and come to a party line vote as a result.

The legislator is also acting in the context of a social group—the legislators. The common tasks, outside criticism, and shared problems create a certain degree of fellowship, depending on the inclusiveness of the legislative involvement and rate of membership turnover. Personal negotiations, mutual back scratching, and efforts at reducing interpersonal conflict are all prominent in the legislative way of life. A willingness to accommodate the other fellow when one's own constituency is indifferent is highly valued. Mutual accommodation is particularly emphasized within the Democratic House Congressional party, where the party loyalty of Congressmen with "uninterested" constituencies is used to support the demands of each of its major "interest" constituencies, thereby further rewarding and reinforcing loyalty. For example, urban Democrats support agricultural subsidies out of party loyalty and a desire to encourage reciprocity on urban programs from rural Democrats.[31]

Since the legislator has usually had some, and often considerable, prior involvement in partisan politics, he brings to the legislature strong party loyalties. Also, he may have worked his way through strong party organizations to this post, and have strong habits and norms of party regularity. (An example of this is provided by New Jersey state legislators.[32]) A disproportionate amount of the political activity of the typical legislator before and after reaching the legislature has been within his own party, thereby reinforcing his personal loyalties and public policy attitudes along partisan lines.[33] Even socialization into the legislature has partisan implications, because friendships form along partisan lines rather than across them. The legislative party is a social group of some significance for this reason.[34]

As a member of the legislature facing reelection the legislator shares a stake in the party's performance. If he is in a marginal district, a poor legislative party record will endanger his seat. If he has a safe seat, the significance of his status in the party leadership or committee leadership will depend heavily on his party's retaining the majority of seats. Hurting the party can have adverse effects on his personal career, even if it does not cost him his seat. It is not surprising that the more cohesive state legislative parties tend to be in the more competitive states.[35]

All of these influences toward partisan behavior (similar effective constituencies, legislative group socialization and partisan recruitment, and common stake in party prestige) create a community of interest among legislators of the same party. This, rather than party discipline, can induce partisan voting in the legislature. The closest approximation of party discipline lies in the usefulness of party machinery to the individual legislator. The party organization can expedite the passage of the legislator's pet bills for his constituency, dispense useful committee assignments, and make necessary information available. In return for these favors, the legislator is quite willing to support the party leadership when strong constituency interests do not require him to vote to the contrary.[36]

The legislative party is relevant and persistent in legislative activity but fluid and factionalized in its organization. As David Truman described the Congressional party, it is a mediate group, a group with which its members have a real but limited involvement. The limitation comes from the decentralization of risks,[37] since the legislator's career is also heavily involved in the constituency and the committees. The involvement is sustained by the converging of many factors which reinforce partisanship without relying on disciplinary powers within the party leadership. A community of interest leads the legislators to parallel and independent decisions, creating a partisan voting pattern. The following section shows the outcome of this balance between factors reducing and enhancing partisanship.

Partisanship in the Legislative Process

A variety of measures of legislative partisanship are available: first vote, roll-call voting, administration program support, and adoption of party platform. How the results of such measures are evaluated depends on the standards and expectations by which one judges legislative voting. Legislative partisanship falls far short of the Party Government prototype, but it demonstrates sufficient consistency to meet the less demanding standards of Responsible Parties.

Legislatures are decisively partisan even if there is only one party line vote per session. The first vote, which selects the presiding officer and organizes the body and its committees on a partisan basis, is the most important vote of the entire session. It is so because it influences all other legislative outcomes by putting different sets of leaders at the control points. These sets of leaders come from distinctively different constituencies and have directly opposing stakes in partisan labels and programs.[38]

The most obvious and easiest way to assess legislative attitudes and activity is by analyzing roll-call votes. There are important limitations to this technique, however.[39] The roll call does not tap the important proceedings prior to voting, especially committee deliberations. Unrecorded votes or activities may be used by legislators to defeat or cripple the bill they later support on the roll call. Nevertheless, the formal vote is the culmination of the legislative process and over a session does not seriously misrepresent the position of most legislators. By these votes, the legislative party defines its position and cohesion.

Legislative voting has been extensively studied, especially in Congress, and some patterns in the results are quite significant for assessing legislative partisanship. A study examining the differences and similarity of the two Congressional parties in the House of Representatives in four sessions from 1921 to 1944 illustrates well the basic situation. Various issues were classified by degree and consistency of partisan cleavage and the following results emerged:

TABLE IX

PARTISAN CLEAVAGE IN CONGRESS BY ISSUE: 1921–44*

Sharp cleavage, consistent:	Tariff, Government Administration, Social and Labor, Farm
Moderate cleavage, consistent:	Government Regulation, Negro, Immigration
Sharp cleavage, inconsistent:	Patronage, Control of House Bureaucracy, Public Works (specific)
Moderate cleavage, inconsistent:	States' Rights, Executive and Congress, Public Works (general), Armaments, Foreign Affairs
Little apparent cleavage:	Veterans' Claims, Women's Rights, District of Columbia, Civil Service, Prohibition

* SOURCE: Julian Turner, *Party and Constituency* (Baltimore, Md.: The Johns Hopkins Press, 1951), p. 70.

Note that issues which have little relation to party program and social composition provide little basis for interparty differences. When the issue depends on being ins or outs (e.g., patronage or public works) the parties are inconsistent, Republicans voting one way when in the majority and another when not, as do the Democrats under similar circumstances. However, when the issues relate to basic party differences in program and political support, the voting differences are consistent. The differences are sharpest when basic liberal versus conservative issues are at stake.

Later studies confirm this pattern. In the 1949–50 session of Congress, voting patterns on Truman Administration bills were tabulated. The heterogeneity of the two parties was reflected in the overlap of support scores, with some liberal Republicans voting more often for the Truman program than some conservative Southern Democrats. Perhaps more striking is the large difference between the average Democrat and the average Republican. The most anti-Truman Democrat supported the administration more often than did the majority of Republicans. There was overlap between the parties because of heterogeneity caused by competitive parties in the quite varied individual states, but this overlap involved relatively few members of each party.[40] An interesting feature of these voting patterns is that the two-party differences were smaller on other, nonadministration bills. The Presidential program provides a focus for and polarization of legislative voting along party lines.[41]

Perhaps the most conclusive demonstration of the importance of legislative partisanship comes in the repeated findings in studies of Congressional behavior that a Congressman's party affiliation is the single best means of predicting his vote. Party affiliation reflects a Congressman's previous career, group memberships, friendship patterns, the nature of his constituency, House organizational links, and probable policy outlook. It is the single fact which tells most about him, more than a characterization of his constituency will.

In state legislatures, the rate of party voting varies quite widely from the almost perfect discipline in Connecticut and New York legislatures to the loose factionalism of Southern legislatures. Party voting is most common where each party is relatively homogeneous and policy oriented, that is, where political polarization is high. The more urbanized and industrialized states create a set of similar constituencies for each party and large differences between the two types of constituency. The competitive impact of a rising minority party also induces more partisan cohesion.[42]

As at the national level, the state administration program brings out a higher level of party voting and two-party difference. Minor nonadministration legislation is more likely to be handled in a routine or nonpartisan manner. When party voting is absent, no other pattern substitutes for it. Ad hoc interest group coalitions may prevail in individual policy sectors. Voting without the influence of party organization does not free the legislator but rather places him adrift in a complex, confused legislative terrain in which the interest groups are helped by their consistency and specificity of effort. The high turnover rates and short sessions of state legislatures make the party a particularly valuable source of coordination and information in state legislative decision-making.[43]

Another test of party performance is the adoption of national party platforms. Contrary to the low popular expectation, roughly three-fourths of the specific platform pledges are fulfilled, with a result similar or equal to what was promised.[44] Since many pledges require executive action and/or executive leadership of the legislature, the party winning the presidency is far more successful than the outs, achieving about four-fifths of its program. But even the defeated party carries out roughly half of its pledges. Not only is an appeal to the party platform a legitimate and persuasive tactic, but also a party platform represents a partisan consensus likely to be reflected in its Congressional delegation and Presidential nominee. Exceptions exist where the critical Congressional groups are remote from the party mainstream, for example, in civil rights legislation and in the case of Southern Democratic Senators. Overall, the existing evidence shows considerable consistency and effort in redeeming party platforms.

If one demands that party lines hold on any and all legislation, then American legislative parties are failures. This very high standard, based on the Party Government prototype, leads to a dismissal of all voting short of 100 per cent differences as meaningless; a viewpoint which attaches more importance to the minority that crosses party lines than to the majority that votes the party position. It is a curious form of mathematics which makes the minority greater than the majority! Such political purity and rigidity is in fact quite inconsistent with the highly pluralistic society and necessarily decentralized political parties of the United States. Why must all minor legislation require the drawing of party lines, when it often has only a marginal relationship to the basic party divisions? Minor modifications of existing administrative organization or highly localized issues need not always call forth the basic socioeconomic alignments that support the major parties.

If the standard of assessment is limited to major legislation, however, and especially to the administration program, then the regularity and cohesion of party voting is more impressive. The administration program and national party platforms represent much better the core of party program than does the entire legislative activity. The essential heterogeneity and limited disciplinary powers of the highly decentralized parties prevent perfect party line voting even on these issues. But the bulk of each party's membership compiles directly opposing voting records. They do so, not because of party discipline, but because of the convergence of many factors creating a community of interest among fellow partisans.[45]

Purists seem unhappy about achieving party voting except by strong party organization and the greater "reliability" of disciplinary means. Their compulsions to tidiness limit their capacity to appreciate the role of the legislative party in achieving considerable coherence and consistency of legislative decision-making in the complex and pluralistic government and society that exists in the United States.

The focus of partisan activity is in the legislative process. However, traces of partisan influence in policy may be found elsewhere. As the judiciary and the bureaucracy share certain important common characteristics here, they can be discussed together.

Nonlegislative Partisanship

Public policy determination is a continuous and multi-stage process, not limited to legislative decisions. The chief executive cannot closely supervise or control most administrative decision-making. The insistence on judicial independence and the power of judicial review grant the courts considerable discretionary authority. Therefore, the differences in general value orientations associated with the basic differences in the social bases and policy orientations of the two parties can lead to different patterns of decision when judges and administrators exercise their discretion.[46] However, it should be noted that partisanship is declining in influence under the impact of growing professionalism and specialization in both the bureaucracy and judiciary.

Whenever a party controls election or appointment to a post, certain systematic differences in the occupants of that post will emerge. The selections of each party will differ in social and economic background of parents, religious and ethnic identification, public policy orientation, partisan recruitment, and the reinforcement of all these by patterns of association paralleling the differences between the two parties.

These value distinctions gain significance from the discretionary choices available to members of the judiciary and the bureaucracy. At the lower levels of both, the accumulation of many minor decisions can have the impact of a policy choice; for example, on questions of a maximum or minimum sentence for violations of gambling laws, or zealous versus lax slum-housing inspections. At the higher levels, choices can restrict and/or expand the scope of public policy; for example, on questions of the constitutionality or judicial interpretation of a state statute regulating business, or an administrative directive spelling out the broad legislation by specific regulations embodying that statute's declaration of public policy.[47]

This is not to say that political parties control the decisions of judges and administrators. Partisanship is only one influence and it is indirect in its effect. The official does not necessarily act consciously as a Republican or Democrat and would very rarely respond to direct orders from his party leader. However, the two parties tend on average to put different men into those offices, men who will make their choices individually and so reflect the differences between the two backgrounds.

Changes have limited the significance of party impact on the judiciary and the bureaucracy, the most important being the growing professionalism of various occupations and specializations, and the doctrines supporting nonpartisan or merit-system selection processes. These changes have important consequences for the political parties and government performance. Professionalism mitigates partisan differences through the sharing of a common training. A profession generates doctrines about how the job must be done and these have public policy implications, for example, the view inculcated in social workers by the schools of social work. In law, the growth of the Bar Associations dominated by high-prestige corporate and civil law practitioners reduces access to the judiciary for a general practice lawyer who is involved in party organization.[48] Prestige and judicial nominations are accorded to specializations remote from party activity and professionalism generally accords status to those who concentrate on their job at the expense of outside involvements, especially political party work. Party organizations are far less likely to have leading professionals in their ranks, and therefore are less able to offer strong candidates for selection to judicial and administrative posts.

Nonpartisan, or merit selection, also favors the exclusion of partisan criteria for appointments. An insulation from politics (to be accurate, partisan politics) leaves the field open to selection by the qualified, that is, the professional groups and other interest groups closely involved with the judicial or administrative task in hand. The legitimacy given expert judgment means that the professions and established interest groups involved will themselves decide who is qualified.

Since these positions wield such discretionary power, it is helpful to find what values are reflected by such professions and interest groups. Nonpartisan selection results in the establishment of élite group values in each of several policy areas, insulated in turn from each other, from party organization, and from the public. Partisan selection, on the other hand, embraces a variety of values and cultures because of the internal diversity of parties, where the élite group taps a relatively narrow range of values.

The professions and their interest group allies may make use of civil service rules, which permit specialist access only, "professional standards," and cries about "spoils" in order to insulate their particular government bureau from both party and chief executive control. The agency then becomes self-governing, reflecting only the values of those with professional status and special claims to knowledge and expertise.[49]

Party influence is declining in the judiciary and bureaucracy, but at the cost of popular control. We have narrower spectrums of values and smaller and narrower aggregations of political actors gaining control of individual governmental bureaus. The administrative branch is fragmented and so rendered less responsive to the chief executive and the popular mandate which he represents. Élite selection and control may be satisfactory to many, but all would be advised to see if they are among those being excluded from the policy choices of these administrators and judges.

The partisan recruitment process provides a crude form of popular consultation by representing a broader spectrum of values than élite selection. Moreover, élite selection tends to magnify the consequences of dispersed authority in the governing structure, whereas partisan appointments help to knit together formally autonomous agencies and permit the extra-legal coordination that might facilitate coordinated and innovative government. Without such assistance, majority rule is limited because of the reduced effectiveness of officials subject to majorities, chief executives and legislative party leaders.

Summary

The pervasiveness of partisanship helps to coordinate government action. It gives meaning to election choices by reinforcing party differences through the processes of recruiting and socializing public officials who have a partisan bias. The consequences are particularly marked in legislatures in which the party organization of communications and agenda is reinforced by the chief executive's policy role. Parties do more than provide channels for policy conflict, because distinctive (although not absolutely different) combinations of policies and concerns are associated with each party.[50] Policy control cannot be detailed, because the basic differences are not precisely defined or applied; rather, on average, there is a greater probability that a Republican will favor a stricter regulation of labor unions, for example. A vague allegiance to a party is therefore an intelligent guide to voter choice in the absence of more detailed information.

Political parties are more significant within the governing process than is often perceived, simply because the alternatives of Party Government and Nonpartisans have dominated the discussion. The obvious failure to achieve Party Government has led people to assume that the opposite is true; yet parties clearly accomplish more than the Status-Quo and Nonpartisan positions would allow. Party membership is only unimportant on minor legislation not closely related to major party divisions. The unevenness of constituency demands creates more slack than the Progressive can accommodate to a direct democracy relationship. So it is the Responsible Parties prototype who comes closest to characterizing American political parties in government. The cumulative impact of recruitment, constituency, and socialization biases enables American political parties to be a strong link between the people and their government and to maintain significant policy differences. The parties are thus intermediary institutions, capable of enhancing the coherence and responsibility of government action.

Each of the preceding five chapters has developed different aspects of party activity; the chapter that follows attempts to relate and integrate these diverse findings.

VII. national executive-centered coalitions

THE DISCUSSION of American political parties usually emphasizes the degree of decentralization in the United States by contrasting the lack of authority in national party leadership to the situation in other countries. On occasion, this view even goes as far as to say that there are no national political parties, only state parties. The sharing of a common label, whether Democrat or Republican, is believed merely to mask the reality of fifty largely autonomous state units.[1] In fact, increasingly during the twentieth century the exact opposite has become more nearly (though not completely) true; there are no state parties, only a national party. To clarify this point it will be necessary to reexamine the characteristics that make up a political party. This chapter therefore emphasizes those factors which give relevance to political parties, rather than the ones which limit their significance. Consequently, the theme of decentralization is deliberately slighted.

The Nature of American Political Parties

A federal system of government and the separation of the executive and legislative branches serve to prevent the development of centralized formal party organizations such as are often found in parliamentary and/or unitary systems of government.[2] The American national conventions are limited in duration and the national committees are essentially powerless.[3] Therefore, seen solely as a formal organization, there is hardly any national party. The formal structure of American political parties is largely defined by state law, which encourages analysts to focus on state parties. However, the current operation of nominating systems, especially the direct primary, and the decline of patronage undercut the meaning of formal organization even at the state level.

While often more influential in their jurisdictions than the national committee may be, the state party committees are not the effective hierarchical superiors of party organizations within their respective states.[4] Decentralization does not stop at the state level, especially since the overthrow of the state nomination convention and the rise of the direct primary in the early twentieth century. In fact, the frequency of cohesive state party organizations has probably been overstated even for the nineteenth century, given the strong role of various urban machines.

In the twentieth century, the likelihood of strong state party organizations has decreased for a variety of reasons. Along with the capacity of United States Senators to lead state party organizations, the potential role of state legislative party caucuses declined after the passage in 1913 of the Seventeenth Amendment.[5] Whereas the state nominating convention permitted central party organization control of the major party decisions, the direct primary transferred influence to major local party strongholds at the expense of the rest of the state party.[6] Unity and coherence are less valuable or likely under the individualist impetus of direct primary campaigns. The direct primary, coupled with the decline of available patronage, have enhanced the possibility of decentralization of the party at every level.[7] The maintenance of formal party organization becomes more difficult and more rare throughout American politics.

But the focus on political parties as formal organizations reflects a bias in expectations about parties. It assumes that parties "should" have identifiable, effective organizations, capable of performing functions necessary in the light of a particular conception of democratic practice. This presumed necessity results from the debate about party prototypes which has defined many of the major concerns for political party analysts; it also derives from the influence of European, especially British, political parties on the standards of assessment.[8]

The limitations on formal organization suggest that a political party might in fact be better understood as an institution, a persistent system of activities and expectations (or any stable pattern of group behavior) rather than as a formal organization. To be precise, an institution in these terms is defined as a "complex normative pattern governing behavior in certain fundamental and recurring situations."[9] The following pages demonstrate the relevance of such a concept to analyzing American political parties correctly.

In order successfully to assert that such a pattern of partisan activities and expectations exists, it will be necessary to establish its structure and what sustains this structure. Certain possibilities can be quickly dismissed. The political party as an institution is not simply the sum of interest group alignments, because interest groups are too diverse, conflicting, and partial in their support of a given party.[10] Ideology involves too few participants and defines too little in American political life to be adequate.[11] Patronage did not fully explain partisan activity even when most available and is a much less useful explanation now.[12]

Nevertheless, certain clues to party structure and its maintenance do exist. One is the persistence of partisan identifications over time, which create influential attitudes in electoral and governing choices.[13] Another is the usefulness of the terminology of coalitions and coalition formation where ordered hierarchies are not possible.[14] These clues indicate that political parties might best be defined thus: *The structure of American political parties as institutions is that of executive-centered coalitions, a coalition of loosely related groupings coordinated by the chief executive's common membership in each group.*[15]

The chief executive is the principal party leader, a first among equals, with limited capacity to command but strategically placed for influence. What principally holds this structure together is partisan identification by individual voters. The party's most significant expression in formal organization is the national nominating convention.[16] Let us now try to demonstrate how the concepts of partisan identification and executive-centered coalition converge to relate a wide variety of "partisan" phenomena and to add up to an identifiable institution.

Partisan Identification

Partisan identification provides the central norm of the institution, because it imposes a pattern on a considerable range of party-related behavior and can do so on a recurring and persistent basis. Not only does three-fourths of the electorate normally have a psychologically effective response to party labels,[17] this response is a factor in a wide variety of offices and elections. Partisanship is not only often a lifetime attribute, but is effectively transmitted to succeeding generations.[18] It remains constantly present among rapidly changing political stimuli. The short-term turnover in political objectives (candidates, specific issues) creates the variety and fluidity of voting choice which is the prime interest of the election analyst, but partisan identification provides much of the stability of the political environment of the average voter.[19]

Partisan identification structures the context in which party leaders, workers, and voters make their choices and thereby leads to partisan patterns of behavior. Party leaders and public officials are not free to make the party anything they choose, but must operate within restraints derived from the expectations resting on partisan identification.[20] Party leadership rests on the effective use of partisanship, for example, conservative Southern Democratic politicians rarely transfer to the Republican party in mid-career. Only the atypical combination of rising Republican Party identification and a large personal following permits and encourages a politician to transfer his party membership successfully, even if he is highly antagonistic to the national party. A rare example of such a change based on these atypical circumstances was provided by Senator Strom Thurmond of South Carolina.

A political party is dependent on partisan identification among the voters through a complex pattern of mechanisms, rather than in a single, invariant relationship. But the following principal mechanisms are usually relevant for a wide range of contexts: common electoral hazards for party leaders and candidates, selective socialization of party cadres, and selective reinforcement of attitudes favorable to partisan choices in electoral and governing decisions.

The partisan tendencies of voters create shared risks for otherwise autonomous elected officials. If, for most officials, the most salient (and often only) fact the voter knows about him is his party affiliation, that knowledge has a strong bearing on the voter's choice.[21] Public officials with competitive or potentially competitive constituencies have at least a small common interest in the prestige of the party label and therefore have incentives toward cooperating to enhance the party performance. The coattail effect of gubernatorial and Presidential candidates on their legislative running mates is one expression of the risks and benefits of partisan response.[22] An individual candidate, especially one running on a lower spot on the ballot, cannot easily differentiate himself from the rest of the party slate and shifting voter evaluations of the party label. A certain amount of party responsibility is in one's individual interest if voters are likely to make collective judgments on party performance, as the "image" evaluations of parties held by voters suggest.[23] Voter awareness of legislative candidates is limited even for Congressional races, and the tendency to follow partisan identification is very strong when such awareness is lacking.[24] Legislators from marginal districts are relatively high in gubernatorial and Presidential support scores, suggesting the linkage of shared risk in the party label.[25] And even party and seniority leaders from safe districts suffer in prestige and influence if their party loses majority control.

The persistence of party identification and its transmission and reinforcement by more immediate social groups maintains a continuity in the social bases of the principal political parties.[26] Group identification usually leads to partisanship consistent with the initial causes of group alignments and current access to party policy. Secular realignments of groups and the resistance of already established partisan identifications will create some discrepancies, for example, Southern Black Republicans in the 1950's. The parties maintain differences in bases of potential voting support, which reinforce the likelihood of distinctive appeals and policy preference by the party.[27] Thus party platforms have consistent differences related to long-standing differences in group support, and these platform differences are consistent with records of performance while in office.[28]

Partisan identification maintains many major policy positions of political parties, but it is not limited to reflecting interest group bases. The partisan identification of a voter also screens his perception of political life, interpreting political events favorably to one's party and thereby reinforcing and strengthening partisan identifications over time.[29]

The party cadres are recruited from among the more partisan segments of the electorate. Active party workers often cite relatives active in politics, group memberships which have partisan relevance, and similar ties as stimulating their initial entry into political activity.[30] Once in the party organization, or active as a candidate or public official, a large share of one's associations and friendships flow along party lines. The initial partisanship is reinforced by close work, dependence on, and friendship with like-minded partisans.[31] This process enhances the possibility of cooperative behavior inside the party group and differentiation from the opposition; note, for instance, that there is a greater difference in policy attitudes between rival party cadres than between nonactive supporters of each party in the electorate.[32] The heightened involvement and information sharpen the degree and awareness of policy conflict.

This socialization creates some degree of common outlook among Republicans or Democrats in all sorts of public and party offices. It enables political parties to reduce the dispersion of authority caused by the separation of powers and federalism. The institutional arrangements do enhance internal party disunity, but the party mechanism is highly useful in moderating the potential for conflict inherent in the American penchant for mechanically balanced government. Partisanship creates a link of common interest (electoral response to party label) and common attitudes (selective party socialization) between officials who would otherwise be highly prone to antagonism because of differing constituencies. So partisans converge within a situation in which they behave similarly, not only because they need to cooperate, but also because they are similar in crucial social attributes, have similar experiences and norms, and, therefore, can independently arrive at similar choices.

This is best demonstrated in the studies of party voting in legislative bodies.[33] Because of the durability and increasingly nationally consistent bases of the political parties, the majority of districts represented by Republicans are likely to be less urban, working-class, Catholic, first- and second-generation American, and Black in population composition than the majority of districts represented by Democrats. The more urbanized, industrialized, and ethnically heterogeneous the state, the greater the similarity of all Republican or all Democratic constituencies and the greater the difference between Democratic and Republican constituencies.[34] The contrast is sharpened by the likelihood that the representative is recruited out of and politically sensitive to the dominant elements of the constituency, those that contribute to its Republican or Democratic propensities.[35]

The direct primary serves to accentuate the similarity of the effective constituencies of Republicans or Democrats still further. The participants in primaries are more deeply partisan than the bulk of the party's electoral support and come disproportionately from party strongholds which are relatively distinctive for each party.[36] Constituency impact on Congressional votes depends on the Congressman's perception of the constituency, which further adds to the importance of the "effective" constituency.[37]

This cumulative bias toward effective constituencies which are distinctively Republican or Democratic tends to align the constituency pressures with the impact of partisan socialization and electoral risks of the party label.[38] This permits strong partisanship in legislatures even though, typically, the disciplinary sanctions available to the legislative party leaders are modest compared to those located in the individual constituency. Yet when the constituencies of a given party are similar in socioeconomic terms, there is a high propensity for party voting. The similarity in backgrounds and experiences leads to parallel choices converging in a single result. Thus, partisanship is the single most explanatory variable of legislative voting patterns in a wide variety of studies.[39]

The modest resources of party leaders are significantly enhanced both by the permissiveness of the constituency on many issues and by the indifference of party program to most parochial issues. The indifference of either the constituency or the party or both gives the legislator considerable discretion on many matters. He is likely to use his discretionary choices to enhance the possibility of favorable treatment by the party or committee leadership on his constituency needs and/or to indulge his own partisan outlook. The permissiveness of his constituency can be used to give the legislator leeway to bargain with party leaders and makes much partisan voting a part of the process of constituency service. The legislator rarely has to choose between constituency and party. Either one or the other is indifferent or they are compatible in most situations.[40]

The differences between the social bases of the two parties are moderated among the political leadership by the advantages of selected middle-class occupational categories, notably lawyers, in pursuing careers in politics; nevertheless, the basic differences do manifest themselves not only in the most directly partisan arenas of party organization—elected executives and legislative positions—but also in other public offices outside these categories. For example, judicial decision patterns reflect the differential recruitment and socialization of partisanship.[41]

Partisan identification among voters and the party cadres provides the link between a Republican in Congress, on the bench, or in the governor's chair. Selective socialization and electoral response are meaningful because of the stability and persistence of partisan identification. This continuity provides an anchor in the political universe, ensuring useful cues for the voter and continuity in the character of the party cadre and leadership. As suggested earlier, the context in which political leaders operate is structured by the electorate as a result of its partisan identification.

Executive-Centered Parties

How does partisan identification ensure that American political parties have an executive-centered coalition structure? The structure could be diffuse, multiple coalitions having no coordinating focus—"coalitions of chieftains," to use another of Dahl's categories.[42] Or it could be focused in the legislature in a cabinet government, such as Hamilton attempted to achieve. How then do chief executives become the center of their parties? The answer lies in their competitive advantages within their own party and the government structure. These advantages are illustrated by the handicaps of the opposition in competing with the incumbent party.

Chief executives have a great advantage over possible rivals in their efforts to coordinate the diverse elements of the party. Both within the party structure and the government structure, the legislative party leaders are handicapped. Within the party, a gubernatorial or Presidential candidate must create a broader coalition than the legislator in order to win either the nomination or the general election. Once elected, the broader range of his coalition enhances his access and tactical possibilities in internal party struggles. The national and state chairmen of incumbent parties are normally selected by, or acceptable to, their respective chief executives. Whatever formal organization exists at the national or state level is therefore amenable to Presidential or gubernatorial influence. The formal apparatus and the legitimacy as titular leader of the party can be utilized to significant, if not decisive advantage. For example, calls for party unity place him at the center of bargaining.

The party primacy of the chief executive lies not only in his advantage in establishing himself as the party leader in the state or nation, but also in the difficulties facing any alternative leader in attempting to do more than limit the impact of his titular status. The loose structure of the party is a coalition which necessarily centers on the chief executive, even though his influence within this coalition may vary widely depending on his skills and opportunities. No other source of party leadership has the legitimacy or the range of sources of influence.

All this is reflected in the superior capacity of the chief executive to define the content of the party label. His initiatives and program define his party in policy terms more effectively than those of any or all other factors. Formal dispersion of governmental authority is characteristic at all levels of government in the United States; innovation calls for broad coalitions and the chief executive is a necessary member of such coalitions. And so public hopes of policy innovation have increasingly come to center on the chief executive.[43] He is advantageously located to exercise initiative through the institutional device of special messages to the legislature, the clearance of administrative agency legislative programs, and the development of the executive budget. The legislative leaders in Congress, and somewhat similarly in state legislatures, are limited by the dispersal of power in the committee system and by relative publicity handicaps; nor can they match the executive resources for initiative. The chief executive's program defines the focus of attention and central controversies of the legislative session.[44] His need to innovate also provides an important motivation for making use of the mechanisms of coordination, of which the political party is the principal one available.

This dependence on the chief executive is illustrated by the fact that his party is more coherent and effective when acting on his legislative program than on other issues.[45] The crucial weakness of the minority party in American politics is the lack of a person or institution able to perform the functions the chief executive provides for the majority party, including giving significance to the national and state party committees, authoritatively defining party policy positions, or establishing coordinated campaign strategies.[46] Opposition majorities in the legislature are negated and relatively ineffectual, as is apparent in David Truman's discussion of "truncated majorities" in Congress.[47] Epitomizing the centrality of the chief executive's position in public perception of political parties is the fact that only 47 per cent of those interviewed at that time knew that the Democrats controlled Congress in 1957–58.[48]

The fact that the opposition party is generally most coherent during a campaign for the election of a chief executive further indicates how much the parties depend on an executive-centered coalition for structure. Off-year elections for either state or national legislative positions break down into a large number of individual, uncoordinated contests. In fact, the growing stature of the defeated Presidential nominee as titular leader has been a key ingredient in the increased coordination of the national opposition's party efforts in the twentieth century;[49] moreover, the increased campaigning effort of the chief executive has modified the off-year elections at the national level.[50]

Both governors and Presidents are therefore effectively the leaders of their respective parties. By their primacy in the coalition, each is better situated than anyone else in their constituencies to limit the decentralization of national and state parties. Each can give his political party a greater coherence than the limits of the party's formal organization and nominating practices would otherwise allow.

National Coalition

The national nominating convention is the tangible organized demonstration of the executive-centered coalition. As a governing body, its powers are limited. Nevertheless, decisions on the seating of delegations can have great impact on nomination outcomes, as was demonstrated during the 1952 Republican battle over the Georgia and Texas delegations. The convention is also a campaign rally, which can whip up the enthusiasm of party workers and bind the participants together in a common zeal for the national party. As a campaign rally it further motivates the partisan sentiments of the general electorate following the convention by television or radio. The platform serves both as a campaign document and as recognition of the diverse factions and issues with which the party is involved. The nomination convention represents and reinforces the diverse national coalition gathered under the party label and sustained by partisan identification.[51]

Above all, the convention centers on the selection of the chief executive of the United States. Both the rules of the Electoral College, and the fact that the presidency is an indivisible prize, make it expedient to form a national coalition in order to pursue that prize. As one observer has noted: "Considered nationally political parties in the United States may be described as loose alliances to win the stakes of power embodied in the presidency."[52]

For these reasons, the national nominating convention is a clear demonstration of the national executive-centered coalition that gives definition to American political parties. Moreover, the national chief executive is far more influential as a party coalition builder and leader than are the governors, because the definition of political parties is made primarily at the national level and by the President. The major party realignments in bases of support and policy orientation have been responses to national events, especially those made more personal by attachments to particular Presidents, e.g., Herbert Hoover and the Republicans as the party of big business and the Depression, and Franklin Delano Roosevelt and the Democrats as the party of the New Deal and prosperity. Group alignments based on these images control much of American voting behavior to this day.[53]

The fundamentally national character of parties is reflected in the fact that partisan identification is almost totally a function of national political events and responses. This is true even in the South where the conflict between the national majority of the Democratic Party and state leadership is most marked, and therefore the hardest possible case. Perception of party policy and definitions of the Democratic Party by the Southern electorate (both white and black) are those pertaining nationally, not locally.[54] The party labels and responses to those labels can only be modestly reshaped from the "givens" provided by the national party. Southern Republicans could not successfully operate as liberal opposition parties to the dominant conservative Democratic leadership in Virginia or Tennessee during the forties and fifties, even though this might have been a rational strategy viewed only in state terms.[55]

Since the partisan label of each legislator determines his vote for the selection of presiding officers and majority control of the committees, conservative Southern Democrats in Congress give their strongest ideological foes resources which negate much of the effectiveness of their later anti-party leadership votes. They are constrained by the partisan identification of their local electorates to limit the scope of their effective opposition by giving the label meaning on the crucial first vote. The significance of partisan identification in conditioning voting decisions leads the Southern electorate to contribute heavily to the election of liberal Democratic Presidents who use the party machinery in Congress to push liberal programs. The use of third parties and unpledged electors as protests by Southern Democrats against the national Democratic Party probably hurt the Republican Party more than the Democratic Party by diffusing anti-administration voting. But these devices enable the state party leaders to retain the advantage of the Democratic Party label.

The failure of efforts to isolate state and national politics from each other by holding state elections in non-Presidential election years is another demonstration of the fundamentally national character of American political parties. The state party favored by the national party allegiances of the state population would continue to win the state elections; the state minority party would be less able to gain office on the basis of temporarily increased national election support.[56] V. O. Key put it best: "The governmental system may be federal but the voter in the polling booth usually is not."[57]

Summary

A particular perspective on American political parties has been outlined above. By defining them as institutions in a non-formal sense, the elements of unity and coherence in partisan activity can be highlighted. Executive-centered coalitions based on partisan identification within the electorate form a mechanism that can pattern expectations and norms about behavior for the party cadre and the electorate. American political parties make much more sense as the result of individual psychological responses to a label than as formal organizations. This concept attempt to link together voting behavior studies, party organization research, and the political party as a policy-forming mechanism in executive-legislative relationships, concerns that are all too often kept far apart.

The most important limitation of this interpretation of American political parties is a temporal one. It is much more relevant and useful in the mid-twentieth century than the late nineteenth century. The decline of formal party organizations and the increasing rate of the chief executive as innovator and coalition leader enhance its descriptive usefulness. These are the changes that most strikingly challenge the traditional conceptions of American political parties.

VIII. conclusion

ALTHOUGH DESCRIBING American political parties as national executive-centered coalitions may help to integrate our current knowledge about partisan activity in its various forms, it leaves two questions unanswered which are important if we are to grasp the full significance of this description. Will the concept continue to be relevant in a period of great change in American politics and political institutions? And what will be the consequences of such political parties in achieving democratic government and realizing any of the party prototypes? On balance, the major trends of the future seem likely to reinforce the national executive-centered coalition aspect of American political parties. They will also support the Responsible Parties prototype, despite institutional and attitudinal limitations on its complete success. The role of political parties in achieving democratic government therefore appears substantial despite notable problems and disadvantages.

Trends and Prospects

Popular pressure for positive government activity shows little prospect of abating; the innovative role of the chief executive should therefore continue to be emphasized. And the continuing decline of formal party organization as material incentives are further reduced should also support the executive-centered aspect of political parties. It is the combination of these two factors, after all, which recently brought this form of party into prominence, and the same combination seems likely to sustain it in the foreseeable future.

The breakdown of what was once a solidly Democratic South reveals that the bases of partisan alignment are increasingly social, decreasingly regional. People in the same social and economic status throughout the country are likely to share similar voting behavior and partisan affiliations.[1] For example, Southern white businessmen are becoming more Republican, like businessmen elsewhere in the nation. Party coalitions are being nationalized by such trends; a declining party heterogeneity will enhance the likelihood of Responsible Parties.

The shift toward national social bases of party support is the result of the New Deal realignment; the collapse of the Solid South is therefore only the final stage of a process which began in the East from the 1928–36 elections. The New Deal realignment of parties continued to expand throughout the post-World War II period, first in the Midwest and now in the South. The growing urbanization and industrialization of regions outside the Northeast supports this trend; in the South, industrialization was accompanied by the migration of Republican Northern middle-class whites into the South, and of working-class blacks out of it. The beginnings of the civil rights movement and the rapid expansion of Southern black voting have also contributed to party realignment.

Party support based on social and economic status increases the relevance of ideological and group-related appeals and encourages support for the national party program. The problem of maintaining party competition in varied jurisdictions prevents overlap and heterogeneity in the national parties from being completely eliminated, but the likelihood of basically right-of-center Republicans facing basically left-of-center Democrats in each individual jurisdiction is enhanced. The lines of political division will become more consistent and widespread. This will again reinforce the national executive-centered coalition at the expense of other elements and increase party responsibility.

A new party realignment could upset this development, but even such an event would not necessarily take party support away from nationalized coalitions. The Republican base of support would most likely be changed by a Southern strategy, which would be a continuation of the trend just discussed, or by expansion through existing social and economic stratifications, reaching deeper into the working class. Entirely new combinations are unlikely or unforeseeable. Moreover, any novel realignment would be a result of national events and policies, which would probably result in nationwide trends in shifting partisan support.

In states generally, the impact of growing operational responsibilities and tax burdens, together with reapportionment and the reform of the executive branch, has sharpened the intensity of party competition and the gubernatorial role. At least twenty-five states can be rated as closely competitive and virtually nowhere can a governor confidently assume reelection. This is a very drastic change of affairs from the situation at the beginning of the twentieth century and the conditions which support it can be expected to continue for at least five to fifteen years. Moreover, the increasing competitiveness of the two parties in most states creates a strong force toward party cohesion, or at least toward more cooperative action and greater party responsibility. Cooperation over either campaigns or governing will enhance the opportunities of the chief executive and help centralization. An example would be cooperative efforts in party finance, which would give new resources to the central party machinery under gubernatorial or Presidential influence.[2]

Party workers will increasingly be recruited from the ideologically motivated as material incentives continue to decline. The Goldwater campaign encouraged this type of recruitment and paid off in greater organization effort by the Republicans in both 1964 and 1968.[3] However, this will tend to reduce leadership flexibility in nominations and enhance the chances of internal party quarrels. To some degree, program consistency and party responsibility will be increased, as the two partisan coalitions become more distinctive in their cadres.

The educational system and the political norms of the middle-class suburbanite will continue to disparage partisanship and boost the Progressive ideology.[4] This ideology and the events of 1968 will probably work to expand and defend the direct primary and the regulation of party organization, thereby limiting the growth of party responsibility.

The general prospect for the national executive-centered coalitions and the Responsible Parties prototype is a positive one, although the increased competitiveness and coherence of political parties will be partially offset by an environment that will continue to remain hostile to partisanship and party organization.[5] Now let us assess the prototypes of American political parties on the basis of this description of party performance.

Party Prototypes and Performance

The national executive-centered coalition most closely resembles the performance expected by the advocates of Responsible Parties. The superiority of Responsible Parties as a description of party performance can be shown by examining American political activity as it meets the requirements of each of our party prototypes, bearing in mind that each of the five prototypes differs in the values it wishes to achieve and in its assessment of the capacities of American political parties.

The Nonpartisan prototype resents democratic, pluralistic decision-making, but the heterogeneous nature of the electorate and its motivations prevent government from being the simple technical application of a common interest and policy that the Nonpartisan viewpoint requires. Popular consultation has to be more complex than that. Moreover, rather than being a nonrational element in politics, the parties are in fact a force for rationalization and coherence of political conflict, using the organizing powers of the party label. Partisanship and party competition increase participation, while Nonpartisan elections decrease participation as the independent voter votes less frequently and is more poorly informed.

The Status-Quo prototype limits majority rule directly and indirectly handicaps popular consultation. Since uncoordinated parties would provide little means for controlling public officials and enforcing responsibility, the value of elections would always be limited. This prototype further underrates partisan identification among the electorate—a factor that makes the parties more meaningful than it anticipates. The continuity and coherence in party program and bases of social group support render the parties more than mere channels for policy conflict, as we have seen. Rather, they function as significant instruments of government.

Party Government advocates demand too much, both in terms of reform of the government structure and of the capacities of the electorate. The concern with issues is limited, variable, and not coherent enough to enable a simple choice between two rival programs. Party government therefore is too much of a Procrustean bed for the heterogeneous population and flexible and diffuse government structure on which Americans pride themselves. Party competition is not close enough or the alternatives simple enough to obtain mandates from elections. Elections are not as well suited to endorsing positive government programs as they are for resisting undesirable policies or rejecting officials. Party Government advocates ask too much of majority rule, and grossly restrict popular consultation.

Progressivism expects too much of the voter in terms of his interest and knowledge. Its reforms (referendum, initiative, recall, and the direct primary) are distorted by low and biased participation. Although his thought may be understandable in a historical context, the Progressive fails to appreciate the positive aspects of party organization and party leadership, and especially neglects the tension between inter-party and intra-party democracy. Operating from a simplistic version of democratic theory, he cannot appreciate the need for intermediate institutions in order to make elections meaningful and officials responsible. Both majority rule and popular consultation need helping hands.

The Responsible Parties prototype accepts the limits provided by the government structure and low levels of voter interest, and concentrates on making the most of responsible government within those limits. Parties differ in their programs and bases of support, but they also overlap so that heterogeneity remains. Partisanship is influential but does not absolutely control the government structure and voter behavior. Other influences work to make the party, the electorate, and the decision-making open and flexible. The pervasiveness of party gives a measure of continuity and coherence to American politics and ensures some distinctiveness and meaning to party candidates and party programs. The shared stake in the party label enables collective responsibility to be the most effective means of achieving the necessary popular consultation.

The central problem to the Responsible Parties prototype is the effectiveness of the minority or out party. The weakness of party competition in many constituencies prevents the minority party from being a credible threat to the restraint of the governing party in many cases. The government structure prevents the outs from having a distinctive center of leadership, which leads to handicaps in planning, public exposure, and political initiative. Since political parties are most coherent and effective as executive-centered coalitions, the opposition party is only adequately mobilized during the general election campaign. It is also handicapped by the consequences of the direct primary for organization activity and recruiting candidates and workers.

The impact of partisanship expressed in national executive-centered coalitions brings the performance of American political parties closest to the Responsible Parties prototype. The low level of issue conceptualization means that the electorate is better able to safeguard its immediate interests, acting as "private partisans," than to mandate positive policy. The diffusion of government authority is ameliorated by partisan ties, but not enough to make Party Government possible; and the Progressive prototype is strongly enough established in election law and public attitudes to prevent complete accomplishment of the Responsible Parties prototype.

Democracy and Parties

American political parties link the diverse concerns of a partially informed electorate to the formation of public policy. Since politics is not spontaneous, it must be organized to render elections meaningful in their impact on public officials and policymaking. Candidates must be recruited and the process of choice simplified by nominations and two-party competition in order to sharpen the blunt tool of the ballot.

Attitudes are organized into two partially different aggregates, but with sufficient continuity and consistency to provide fixed points of reference for the voter. Republicans and Democrats do enough different things while in office to make the choice significant for the voter. Most of the blurring of party lines is a result of government decentralization, through federalism and separated branches, and party decentralization through the direct primary. The lack of ideology and of well-defined party programs is a consequence of the voter's indifference to ideology and his lack of structured opinions on related issues.

The party label provides the marginally involved citizen with a means of assigning responsibility for unfavorable government acts, or with a general response to the current administration, without his having to have a detailed knowledge of current political events. Political parties therefore compensate for the low level of information and interest of the average voter. Without them, voting choices and public policy would be far more random and irrational.

Political parties are the principal mechanism of government available to popular majorities. Only through the minority party's capacity to create an effectively organized competition can elections be made meaningful and public officials responsive to the public will. The parties have the widespread influence necessary to innovate within the government structure with multiple veto points. Because the executive is necessary to this innovation, the parties are executive-centered coalitions.

But the degree of achievement and potential for achievement should not be equated with actual accomplishment. Not only do national executive-centered coalitions and responsible parties fall somewhat short of democratic standards in practice, they are also only part of a larger social, political, and economic system which controls the performance of parties and contributes directly to the possibility of democratic government. For example, we have seen that partisan identification is important because of the low issue involvement of the general public. The low priority of political affairs means that social processes rather than direct political experiences influence allegiances and issue perspectives more heavily. Moreover, the social and economic inequalities lead to inequality in opportunities for political participation, thereby preventing political equality.

A generous assessment of political parties in America would stress what they accomplish toward democratic government, despite the many restrictions on party performance and the inhibitions on effective political participation of the disadvantaged. But it is not enough to say that political parties can serve egalitarian ends. What we need is further effort to ensure that party performance is more consistently responsible, by broadening the popular base and democratic representativeness of party organization. More widespread and consistent popular participation in the slack, undermanned party organizations will enhance the sensitivity of party nominations and leaders to new issues and events at all levels of government. The biases of Progressivism must be overcome if we are to ensure more responsible parties.

notes

Chapter I. Democratic Theory and Political Parties

1. The following discussion relies directly and heavily on the excellent summary of the theory of democratic government found in Austin Ranney and Willmore Kendall, *Democracy and the American Party System* (New York: Harcourt, Brace & Co., 1956), Chapters 1–6. Also of considerable value is Henry B. Mayo, *An Introduction to Democratic Theory* (New York: Oxford University Press, 1960) and Stanley I. Benn and Richard S. Peters, *The Principles of Political Thought* (New York: The Free Press, 1965), especially Chapter 15.

2. Benn and Peters, *op. cit.*, p. 393.

3. *Ibid.*, p. 413.

4. Ranney and Kendall, *op. cit.*, pp. 23–37.

5. Robert A. Dahl, *A Preface to Democratic Theory* (Chicago: University of Chicago Press, Phoenix Books, 1963), pp. 124–33.

6. Ranney and Kendall, *op. cit.*, pp. 42–54.

7. See Robert C. Wood, *Surburbia* (Boston: Houghton Mifflin Co., 1959) and James W. Fesler, "Approaches to the Understanding of Decentralization," *Journal of Politics,* XXVII (August 1965), pp. 536–66.

8. John Locke, "Of the Extent of the Legislative Power" and "Of the Legislative, Executive and Federative Power of the Commonwealth," Chapters XI and XII of *The Second Treatise of Civil Government,* in Thomas I. Cook (ed.), *Two Treatises of Government* (New York: Hafner Publishing Co., 1947), pp. 188–96.

9. Jean Jacques Rousseau, *The Social Contract,* ed. G. D. H. Cole (New York: E. P. Dutton and Co., Inc., 1950) Book III, Chapter IV, pp. 64–66.

10. Avery Leiserson, *Parties and Politics* (New York: Alfred A. Knopf, Inc., 1958), pp. 42–43.

11. Ranney and Kendall, *op. cit.,* Chapter 6.

12. The leading spokesmen for this school are E. E. Schattschneider, *Party Government* (New York: Holt, Rinehart and Winston, Inc., 1942) and James M. Burns, *The Deadlock of Democracy* (Englewood Cliffs, N.J.: Prentice-Hall, Inc., 1963), Chapters 9, 10, and 14. "Toward a More Responsible Two-Party System," *American Political Science Review,* XLIV, Supplement (September 1950) summarizes this outlook in a committee report. All the above were drawn upon for the arguments that follow.

13. V. O. Key, Jr., was the most representative spokesman of this school of thought. The sweeping reforms and goals of party government are subordinated to increasing responsibility within the existing institutional structure. *Cf. Parties, Politics and Pressure Groups,* 5th ed. (New York: Thomas Y. Crowell Co., 1964).

14. V. O. Key, Jr., *The Responsible Electorate* (Cambridge, Mass.: Belknap Press, 1966), pp. 76–77.

15. David B. Truman, "Federalism and the Party System" in Arthur Macmahon (ed.), *Federalism: Mature and Emergent* (Garden City, N.Y.: Doubleday and Co., Inc., 1955), pp. 116–34.

16. Stressed in V. O. Key, Jr., *American State Politics* (New York: Alfred A. Knopf, Inc., 1957).

17. Allen Nevins, "The Strength of Our Political System," *The New York Times Magazine* (July 18, 1948), p. 5, illustrates the rationale of this position, as does Ranney and Kendall, *op. cit.,* Chapters 20–22, especially pp. 514–25.

18. Pendleton Herring, *The Politics of Democracy* (New York: Rinehart & Co., 1940), pp. 100–6.

19. A leading example of Progressive thought, Herbert Croly, is analyzed by Austin Ranney, *The Doctrine of Responsible Party Government* (Urbana, Ill.: The University of Illinois Press, 1962), Chapter 8.

20. Ranney and Kendall, *op. cit.,* pp. 118–29.

21. Ranney, *The Doctrine of Responsible Party Government,* Chapter 7.

22. Charles R. Adrian, "Some General Characteristics of Non-partisan Elections," *American Political Science Review,* XLVI, No. 3 (September 1952), pp. 766–76, and Robert R. Alford and Eugene C. Lee, "Voting Turnout in American Cities," *American Political Science Review,* LXII, No. 3 (September 1968) pp. 796–813.

Chapter II. Competition

1. Leon D. Epstein, "A Comparative Study of Canadian Parties," *American Political Science Review,* LVIII, No. 1 (March 1964), pp. 48–50.

2. *Ibid.*

3. Frank J. Sorauf, *Political Parties in the American System* (Boston: Little, Brown and Company, 1964), pp. 27–32.

4. *E.g.,* Thomas B. Littlewood, *Bipartisan Coalition in Illinois* (New York: McGraw-Hill Book Company, 1960).

5. Schattschneider, *Party Government,* pp. 74–84.

6. V. O. Key, Jr., *Southern Politics* (New York: Alfred A. Knopf, Inc., 1950), pp. 416–23.

7. Maurice Klain, "A New Look at the Constitutencies," *American Political Science Review,* XLIX, No. 4 (December 1955), pp. 1105–19. Reapportionment in the 1960's did not modify this proportion; 44.7% of all state legislative seats were in multi-member districts in 1968, *The Book of the States: 1968–69,* Vol. XVII (Chicago: The Council of State Governments, 1968), pp. 41, 66–7.

8. Douglas Rae, *The Political Consequences of Electoral Laws* (New Haven, Conn.: Yale University Press, 1967), pp. 134–40.

9. William N. Chambers, *Political Parties in a New Nation* (New York: Oxford University Press, 1963), pp. 31, 127, 161.

10. Giovanni Sartori, "European Political Parties: The Case of Polarized Pluralism," in Joseph La Palombara and Myron Weiner (eds.) *Political Parties and Political Development,* (Princeton, N.J.: Princeton University Press, 1966), pp. 137–76.

11. Immanuel Wallerstein, "The Decline of the Party in Single-Party African States," in *ibid.,* pp. 203–6.

12. William N. Chambers, "Party Development and the American Mainstream," in William N. Chambers and Walter D. Burnham (eds.), *The American Party Systems* (New York: Oxford University Press, 1967), pp. 24–8; and Ranney and Kendall, *Democracy and the American Party Systems,* pp. 470–77. The existence of a consensus beyond the vaguest of beliefs is highly controversial, but the contrast to the severe class and ideological conflict in many western European countries makes it credible on a very crude comparative basis.

13. Stokely Carmichael and Charles V. Hamilton, *Black Power* (New York: Random House, Inc., Vintage Books, 1967), Chapter 5.

14. Lewis A. Froman, Jr., *Congressmen and Their Constituencies* (Chicago: Rand McNally and Co., 1963), p. 62.

15. John H. Fenton, *Midwest Politics* (New York: Holt, Rinehart and Winston, Inc., 1960), pp. 9–15, 48–54, 89–93.

16. Austin Ranney, "Parties in State Politics," in Herbert Jacob and Kenneth N. Vines (eds.), *Politics in the American States* (Boston: Little, Brown and Co., 1965), pp. 63–67.

17. Only 22 per cent of the House districts have even had the two parties represented from 1952 to 1962, Froman, *op. cit.,* pp. 61–62.

18. Malcolm E. Jewell, "The Political Setting," in Alexander Heard (ed.), *State Legislatures in American Politics* (Englewood Cliffs, N.J.: Prentice-Hall, Inc., 1966), pp. 75–77.

19. *Ibid.,* pp. 77, 81–82.

20. The typology and best summary discussion of minor parties is found in Key, *Politicis, Parties and Pressure Groups,* Chapter 10.

21. *Ibid.,* p. 274.

22. *Ibid.,* pp. 274–77.

23. *Ibid.,* pp. 278–81.

24. Robert B. Semple, Jr., *The New York Times,* Sept. 21, 1968, 17:2.

25. Recent examples include Richard L. Strout, "Next Year A Funny Thing Could Happen on the Way to the White House," *The New York Times Magazine,* July 23, 1963, pp. 24–25. The most thorough consideration of the contingencies involved is by Russell Baker, "The Picking of the President, 1968," *The Saturday Evening Post,* Vol. 241, No. 5 (March 9, 1968), pp. 19 ff; and Neal R. Peirce, *The People's President* (New York: Clarion Books, 1968).

26. *The New York Times,* Nov. 4, 1968, 1:7.

27. James C. Kirby, Jr., "Turmoil on the Electoral College Campus," *The Progressive,* XXXII, No. 10 (October 1968), pp. 13–17.

28. Louis Harris poll reported in *The New York Times,* Sept. 5, 1967, 28:2, and analyzed by Richard M. Scammon, "How Wallace Will Run His Third-Party Campaign," *The Reporter,* XXXVII, No. 6 (Oct. 19, 1967), pp. 34–36. Harris poll reported in *The New York Times,* Nov. 3, 1967, 28:8, shows that the GOP loss occurs both in the South and the North. Another Harris poll reported in *Washington Post,* July 15, 1968, A4:1, showed the same pattern, as did *The New York Times,* Jan. 31, 1969. 20:4.

29. Interview with George Wallace, *The New York Times,* Nov. 10, 1968, 55:1.

30. Senator Thurmond was able to make the switch because he had an exceptionally large personal following. He did so with great public exposure at a time when the Republican Party had become sufficiently well established that its electoral base combined with his personal following could provide a majority. Senator Wayne Morse of Oregon made the shift in the opposite direction with a similar following and public

exposure to a rising state Democratic Party. A new development in 1968 was an offer to protect the seniority of Congressional Democrats bolting to Republicans, *The New York Times,* Sept. 20, 1968, 32:2.

31. Neil R. Peirce, "The Electoral College Goes to Court," *The Reporter,* XXXV, No. 2 (Oct. 6, 1966), pp. 34–37.

32. Sixty-three per cent endorsed direct election in a 1966 Gallup poll, Pierce, *ibid.,* pp. 34–7, and 66 per cent in a 1968 Gallup poll, *The New York Times,* Sept. 22, 1968, 61:1.

33. Key, *Southern Politics,* pp. 416–23.

34. U. S. Bureau of Census, *Historical Statistics of the United States,* pp. 682–83.

Chapter III. The Limits on Party Organization

1. American Political Science Association, *Toward a More Responsible Two-Party System,* Chapter 8.

2. This argument is more fully developed by Joseph A. Schlesinger, "Political Party Organizations," in James G. March (ed.), *Handbook of Organizations* (Chicago: Rand McNally & Co., 1965), pp. 764–801; *see also* his *Ambition and Politics* (Chicago: Rand McNally & Co., 1967).

3. James A. Riedel, "Boss and Faction," *The Annals of the American Academy of Political and Social Science,* Vol. 353 (May 1964), pp. 14–26.

4. William N. Chambers, "Party Development and the American Mainstream," *The American Party Systems,* pp. 3–32.

5. Jack Dennis, "Support of the Party System by the Mass Public," *American Political Science Review,* LX, No. 3 (September, 1966), pp. 600–15.

6. Key, *American State Politics,* pp. 56–57.

7. James Q. Wilson and Peter B. Clark, "Incentive Systems: A Theory of Organizations," *Administrative Science Quarterly,* VI, No. 2 (September 1961), pp. 129–66, provide the typology of incentives being used below.

8. A defense of the Tweed Ring along these lines is found in Seymour J. Mandelbaum, *Boss Tweed's New York* (New York: John Wiley & Sons, Inc., 1965).

9. Frank R. Kent, *The Great Game of Politics* (Garden City, N.Y.: Doubleday, Doran and Company, Inc., 1935), pp. 56–57, and *passim.*

10. Carl R. Fish, *The Civil Service and the Patronage* (New York: Russell and Russell, Inc., 1963), pp. 229–36.

11. Frank J. Sorauf, "The Silent Revolution in Patronage," *Public Administration Review,* XX, No. 1 (Winter 1960), pp. 28–34.

12. Wilson and Clark, "Incentive Systems," discusses normative and social incentives more extensively; also James Q. Wilson, *The Amateur Democrat* (Chicago: University of Chicago Press, 1962), Chapter 5; and M. Margaret Conway and Frank B. Feigert, "Motivation, Incentive Systems, and the Political Party Organization," *American Political Science Review,* LXII, No. 4 (December 1968), pp. 1159–73.

13. Key, *Southern Politics,* p. 292.

14. Key, *Politics, Parties and Pressure Groups,* pp. 373–76.

15. *The Book of the States,* 1966–69, Vol. XVII (Chicago: The Council of State Governments, 1968), p. 23. Additionally, Republicans can use conventions in a number of Southern states, and Iowa and South Dakota have post-primary conventions if the leading candidate receives less than 35 per cent of the primary vote.

16. Frank J. Sorauf, *Party and Representation* (New York: Atherton Press, 1963), pp. 43-62.

17. Key, *Politics, Parties and Pressure Groups,* p. 378.

18. Key, *American State Politics,* pp. 155-61.

19. *Ibid.,* pp. 171-93.

20. Some feel that Key's argument about the nonrepresentative character of primary elections is incorrect: Austin Ranney and Leon D. Epstein, "The Two Electorates: Voters and Non-Voting in a Wisconsin Primary," *The Journal of Politics,* XXVIII, No. 3, (August, 1966), pp. 598-616, and Austin Ranney, "The Representativeness of Primary Electorates," *Midwest Journal of Political Science,* XII, No. 2 (May, 1968), pp. 224-38. But the demonstration of issue similarity between voters and nonvoters was either very indirect or in a primary lacking a strong issue stimulus. Both articles show striking differences between voters and nonvoters in politically relevant attributes, such as socioeconomic status, political involvement, and partisan activity, plus mixed results on intensity of partisan identification. In any event, a variety of states will need to be studied to settle the question.

21. *The New York Times,* Sept. 25, 1968, 28:2.

22. Allan P. Sindler, "Bifactional Rivalry as an Alternative to Two-Party Competition in Louisiana," *American Political Science Review,* XLIX (September 1955), pp. 641-62.

23. Schattschneider, *op. cit.,* pp. 74-84.

24. Fenton, *op. cit.,* pp. 62-63 and 86-87.

25. The openness of the minority is argued by Theodore Lowi, "Toward Functionalism in Political Science: The Case of Innovation in Party Systems," *American Political Science Review,* LVII, No. 3 (September 1963), pp. 570-83.

26. Duane Lockard, *Connecticut's Challenge Primary* (New York: McGraw-Hill Book Company, 1960).

27. C. A. Berdahl, "Party Membership in the United States," *American Political Science Review,* XXXVI (1942), pp. 16-50, 241-62.

28. See Francis Carney, *The Rise of the Democratic Clubs in California* (New York: McGraw Hill Book Company, 1960); Leon D. Epstein, *Politics in Wisconsin* (Madison, Wisc.: University of Wisconsin Press, 1958); and Wilson, *The Amateur Democrat,* Chapter 4.

29. Stanley Kelley, Jr., Richard E. Ayres, and William G. Brown, "Registration and Voting: Putting First Things First," *American Political Science Review,* LXI, No. 2 (June, 1967), pp. 359-79; also William G. Andrews, "American Voting Participation," *Western Political Quarterly,* XIX, No. 4 (December 1966), pp. 639-52.

30. Key, *Politics, Parties and Pressure Groups,* Chapter 23, and Kent, *op. cit.,* pp. 14-8.

31. Alexander Heard, *The Costs of Democracy* (Garden City, N.Y.: Doubleday and Company, Inc., 1962), pp. 227-48.

Chapter IV. Voters and Partisanship

1. An excellent illustration of the problem of perception is found in the 1964 Goldwater campaign as analyzed by Philip E. Converse, Aage R. Clausen, and Warren E. Miller, "Electoral Myth and Reality: 1964 Election," *American Political Sicence Review,* LIX, No. 2 (June 1955), pp. 321-36.

2. Angus Campbell, Philip E. Converse, Warren E. Miller, and Donald E. Stokes, *The American Voter* (New York: John Wiley and Sons, Inc., 1960), p. 17. *The American Voter* and related studies have provided major breakthroughs in the understanding of electoral behavior and will be relied on heavily.

3. *Ibid.,* p. 67.

4. *Ibid.,* p. 74.

5. *Ibid.,* pp. 77–86; the concept of cross pressures originally developed by Paul F. Lazarsfeld, Bernard Berelson, and Hazel Gaudet, *The People's Choice* (New York: Columbia University Press, 1944).

6. Donald Stokes, "Some Dynamic Elements of Contests for the Presidency," *American Political Science Review,* LX, No. 1 (March 1966), pp. 19–28.

7. Campbell, *et. al., op. cit.,* pp. 44–50, 300–14; and Bernard Berelson, Paul F. Lazarsfeld, and William McPhee, *Voting* (Chicago: University of Chicago Press, 1954), pp. 88–117.

8. Campbell, *et. al., op. cit.,* pp. 553–56.

9. Stokes, *op. cit.,* pp. 20–21.

10. Converse, Clausen, and Miller, "Electoral Myth and Reality," p. 331.

11. *Ibid.,* pp. 21–2.

12. *The New York Times,* Sept. 8, 1968, 77:4; and Oct. 30, 1968, 22:4.

13. Converse, Clausen, and Miller, "Electoral Myth and Reality," pp. 26–7.

14. *Ibid.,* p. 22; and Philip E. Converse, Angus Campbell, and Warren E. Stokes, "Stability and Change in 1960: A Reinstating Election," *American Political Science Review,* LV, No. 2 (June 1961), pp. 269–80.

15. Stokes, *op. cit.,* p. 22; in 1968, Nixon was favored over Humphrey in personal comparisons, Gallup Poll, *New York Times,* Sept. 25, 1968, 29:1.

16. Stokes, *op. cit.,* pp. 24–26.

17. An excellent analysis of this variation is found in Ithiel deSola Pool, Robert P. Abelson, and Samuel Popkin, *Candidates, Issues and Strategies* (Cambridge, Mass.: The Massachusetts Institute of Technology Press, 1964), pp. 64–126.

18. *Ibid.,* p. 27.

19. Campbell, *et. al., op. cit.,* pp. 121–28.

20. Based on tables on change in partisan identification in Angus Campbell, Philip E. Converse, Warren E. Miller, and Donald E. Stokes, *Elections and the Political Order* (New York: John Wiley & Sons, Inc., 1966), p. 238, and Campbell, *et. al., The American Voter,* p. 148, Table 7.2. This argument is more fully developed by Gerald Pomper, "Classification of Presidential Elections," *Journal of Politics,* XXIX, No. 3 (August 1967), pp. 558–60.

21. Philip E. Converse, "The Concept of a Normal Vote," in Campbell, *et. al., Elections and the Political Order,* pp. 12–27.

22. *Ibid.,* p. 27–30.

23. Campbell, *et. al., The American Voter,* pp. 143–45.

24. Key, *The Responsible Electorate,* pp. 9–28.

25. Campbell, *et. al., The American Voter,* pp. 146–48; and Berelson, *et. al., Voting,* pp. 88–117.

26. Campbell, *et. al., The American Voter,* p. 99.

27. *Ibid.,* pp. 101–6.

28. Converse, Clausen, and Miller, *op. cit.,* p. 323.

29. Campbell, *et. al., Elections and the Public Order,* pp. 27–30, and Edgar Litt, "Civic Education, Community Norms, and Political Indoctrination," *American Sociological Review,* XXVIII (February 1963), pp. 69–75.

30. U.S. Bureau of Census, *Historical Statistics of the United States, Colonial Times to 1957,* (Washington, D.C.: U.S. Printing Office, 1960), p. 683.

31. *Ibid.,* p. 682. This is also confirmed by Pomper, "Classification of Presidential Elections," p. 544; his analysis singles out 1928 as the most critical election in this group in further realignment.

32. Campbell, *et. al., The American Voter,* pp. 283-9, and Jack L. Walker, "Ballot Forms and Voter Fatigue: An Analysis of the Office Block and Party Column Ballots," *Midwest Journal of Political Science,* X, No. 4 (November 1966), pp. 448-63.

33. Campbell, *et. al., The American Voter,* pp. 133-41.

34. *Ibid.,* p. 132.

35. V. O. Key, Jr. has examined the persistence of sectional patterns in various states. A good example is "Partisanship and County Office: The Case of Ohio," *American Political Science Review,* XLVII (June 1953), pp. 525-32.

36. John H. Fenton, *Midwest Politics* (New York: Holt, Rinehart & Winston, 1966), pp. 155-63.

37. Key, "Partisanship and County Office."

38. Berelson, *et. al., Voting,* pp. 54-76.

39. Ralph A. Straetz and Frank Munger, *New York Politics* (New York: Citizenship Clearing House, 1960), pp. 55-57.

40. The most important examples of the literature on the early stages of developing political attitudes are in Herbert Hyman, *Political Socialization* (Glencoe, Ill.: The Free Press, 1959), and Fred I. Greenstein, *Children and Politics* (New Haven: Yale University Press, 1966).

41. Campbell, *et. al., The American Voter,* pp. 146-48.

42. *Ibid.,* pp. 307-10.

43. *Ibid.,* pp. 330-31.

44. *Ibid.,* pp. 370-72.

45. *Ibid.,* pp. 356.

46. *Ibid.,* pp. 153-56.

47. *Ibid.,* pp. 459-60.

48. *Ibid.,* p. 150.

49. *Ibid.,* p. 489-93.

50. Wood, *Suburbia,* pp. 135-53; and Campbell, *et. al., The American Voter,* pp. 455-71.

51. Campbell, *et. al., The American Voter,* pp. 169-71.

52. Campbell, *et. al., The American Voter,* pp. 153-56; and Gallup poll reported in *The New York Times,* April 10, 1968, 27:3.

53. *Ibid.,* pp. 172-74.

54. *Ibid.,* pp. 50-51.

55. Berelson, *et. al., Voting,* pp. 218-22. The complexity of the relation of public opinion to parties is further indicated by findings which suggest that the closest relation between voting preference and policy positions occurs in states where party cohesion and competition is intermediate, rather than high or low, Charles F. Cnudde, "Public Opinion in the States," in (ed.) Robert E. Crew, Jr., *State Politics* (Belmont, Calif.: Wadsworth Publishing Co., Inc., 1968), pp. 165-84.

56. Campbell, *et. al., The American Voter,* p. 184.

57. *Ibid.,* p. 195, and V. O. Key, Jr., *Public Opinion and American Democracy* (New York: Alfred A. Knopf, Inc., 1961), pp. 153–63.

58. Key, *Public Opinion and American Democracy,* pp. 163–72; and Robert Axelrod, "The Structure of Public Opinion on Policy Issues," *Public Opinion Quarterly,* XXXI, No. 1 (Spring 1967), pp. 51–60.

59. Campbell, *et. al., The American Voter,* pp. 197–200.

60. *Ibid.,* pp. 201–3, and Key, *The Responsible Electorate, ad passim.*

61. Campbell, *et. al., The American Voter,* pp. 205–7.

62. *Ibid.,* pp. 227–50, 397–400.

63. Converse, Clausen, and Miller, *op. cit.,* p. 335; but it did change party images, as will be discussed in Chapter V.

64. Campbell, *et. al., The American Voter,* p. 251.

65. Eugene Burdick, "Political Theory and the Voting Studies," in (ed.) Eugene Burdick and Arthur Bradbeck *American Voting Behavior* (Glencoe, Ill.: The Free Press, 1959), pp. 136–49.

Chapter V. Campaigns and Elections

1. Gerald Pomper, "The Concept of Elections in Democratic Theory," *The Review of Politics,* XXIX, No. 4 (October, 1967), pp. 478–91.

2. Stanley Kelley, Jr., *Professional Public Relations and Political Power* (Baltimore: The John Hopkins Press, 1956), pp. 26–38.

3. Heard, *The Costs of Democracy,* pp. 264–72.

4. *Ibid.,* pp. 227–48.

5. White, *The Making of the President,* 1960, pp. 109–12; and Harry W. Ernst, *The Primary That Made a President: West Virginia 1960* (New York: McGraw-Hill Book Company, 1962).

6. Heard, *The Costs of Democracy,* pp. 17–34.

7. *Ibid.,* Chapter 12; and Tom Wicker, *The New York Times,* May 27, 1967, 14:4.

8. Murray Levin, *The Compleat Politician* (Indianapolis: Bobbs-Merrill, 1962), pp. 183–87; and John H. Kessel, "A Game Theory Analysis of Campaign Strategy," (ed.) M. Kent Jennings and L. Harmon Zeigler, *The Electoral Process* (Englewood Cliffs, N.J.: Prentice-Hall, Inc., 1966), pp. 298–302.

9. Levin, *op. cit.,* pp. 192–93; Louis Harris, "Polls and Politics in the United States, *Public Opinion Quarterly,* XXVII, No. 1 (Spring, 1963), pp. 3–8; and Pool, Abelson, and Popkin, *Candidates, Issues and Strategies, op. cit.,* which discusses simulation. Polls are increasingly used to encourage campaign contributions in close races, *The New York Times,* November 7, 1966, 23:1.

10. Charles Peabody's campaign for the 1960 Democratic nomination for Governor of Massachusetts was led astray by bad polling, Levin, *op. cit.,* pp. 188–89.

11. John Bibby and Roger Davidson, *On Capital Hill* (New York: Holt, Rinehart & Winston, Inc., 1967), pp. 38–39.

12. Edward N. Costikyan, *Behind Closed Doors* (New York: Harcourt, Brace and World, 1966), pp. 240–52.

13. David O. Sears and Jonathan L. Freedman, "Selective Exposure to Information: A Critical Review," *Public Opinion Quarterly,* XXXI, No. 2 (Summer, 1967), pp. 194–213.

14. The best general discussions of campaign strategies are found in Lewis A. Froman, Jr., "A Realistic Approach to Campaign Strategies and Tactics," in Jennings and Zeigler, eds., *The Electoral Process,* pp. 1–19; Kessel, "A Game Theory Analysis of Campaign Strategy," pp. 290–303; and Kelley, *Professional Public Relations and Political Power.*

15. Froman, "A Realistic Approach to Campaign Strategies and Tactics," pp. 11–14, 16.

16. Phillips Cutright and Peter H. Rossi, "Grass Roots Politicians and the Vote," *American Sociological Review,* XXIII, (April, 1958), pp. 171–79, and "Party Organization in Primary Elections," *American Journal of Sociology,* LXIV (November 1958), pp. 262–9, and Daniel Katz and Samuel J. Eldersveld, "The Impact of Local Party Activity Upon the Electorate," *Public Opinion Quarterly,* XXV (Spring 1961), pp. 1–24.

17. *The New York Times,* May 25, 1965, 1:6; June 5, 1965, 18:1, 8; June 28, 1965; 1:2; Sept. 1, 1965, 23:4; and Nov. 15, 1965, 32:3.

18. Elihu Katz and Paul F. Lazarsfeld, *Personal Influence* (New York: The Free Press of Glencoe, Inc., 1955); David B. Truman, *The Governmental Process* (New York: Alfred A. Knopf, Inc., 1958), pp. 195–98; and Campbell, *et. al., The American Voter,* pp. 218–20.

19. There is also the problem suggested by Heard, *op. cit.,* p. 262, that planning a campaign in the mass media often needs to start before the candidates are chosen, which makes it difficult to shorten the campaign period.

20. Charles O. Jones, "The Role of the Campaign in Congressional Politics," in Jennings and Zeigler (eds.), *The Electoral Process,* pp. 21–22.

21. Donald Stokes and Warren Miller, "Party Government and the Saliency of Congress," *Public Opinion Quarterly,* XXVI (Winter 1962), pp. 541.

22. Jones, "The Role of the Campaign in Congressional Politics," pp. 28–34.

23. The significance of strong party organization for recruitment is explored by Leo M. Snowiss, "Congressional Recruitment and Representation," *American Political Science Review,* LX, No. 3 (September 1966), pp. 627–39.

24. *E.g.,* Speakers Champ Clark in 1912 and John Nance Garner in 1932.

25. Julius Turner, "Primary Elections as the Alternative to Party Competition in 'Safe' Districts," *Journal of Politics,* XV (May 1953), pp. 197–210.

26. Jones, *op. cit.,* p. 24; and H. Douglas Price, "The Electoral Arena," in (ed.) David B. Truman, *The Congress and America's Future* (Englewood Cliffs, N.J.: Prentice-Hall, Inc., 1965), pp. 42–5.

27. Jewell, *op. cit.,* pp. 33–45.

28. Barbara Hinckley, "Interpreting House Mid-Term Elections," *American Political Science Review,* LXI, No. 3 (September 1967), pp. 694–700.

29. *Ibid.;* Angus Campbell, "Surge and Decline," *Elections and the Electoral Order,* pp. 40–62; and "Voters and Elections: Past and Present," *Journal of Politics,* XXVI (November 1964), pp. 745–57.

30. *E.g.,* David B. Truman, *The Congressional Party* (New York: John Wiley & Sons, Inc., 1959), pp. 216–19.

31. Paul T. David, "The Changing Political Parties," *Continuing Crisis in American Politics,* in (ed.) Marian D. Irish (Englewood Cliffs, N.J.: Prentice-Hall, Inc., 1963), pp. 56–57.

32. Miller and Stokes, "Constituency Influence in Congress," *American Political Science Review,* LVII (March 1963), pp. 45–56.

33. Oliver Garceau and Corrine Silverman, "A Pressure Group and the Pressured," *American Political Science Review,* XLVIII (September 1954), pp. 672–91, and Lewis A. Dexter, "The Representative and His District," *Human Organization,* XVI (1957), pp. 2–13.

34. John W. Kingdon, "Politicians' Beliefs About Voters," *American Political Science Review,* LXI, No. 1 (March 1967), pp. 137–45.

35. Gerald Pomper, *Nominating the President* (New York: W. W. Norton, 1966), pp. 8–9.

36. Gallup poll reported in *The New York Times,* September 22, 1968, 61:1.

37. The leading accounts on the national party conventions are found in Paul T. David, Ralph M. Goldman, and Richard C. Bain, *The Politics of National Party Conventions* (Washington, D.C.: The Brookings Institution, 1960), and Pomper, *Nominating the President.* Both were relied on below.

38. California is a major exception to these points: Pomper, *Nominating the President,* pp. 42–48, 106–110.

39. *Ibid.,* pp. 110–14; Ernest, *The Primary That Made a President;* and James W. Davis, *Presidential Primaries* (New York: Thomas Y. Crowell, 1967), pp. 1–14.

40. Pomper, *Nominating the President,* pp. 116–18, 267–68; and White, *The Making of the President 1964,* p. 118, discuss Goldwater's partisan work. A poll of Democratic county chairmen prior to the 1968 convention indicated that 70 per cent favored Humphrey, *The New York Times,* June 2, 1968, 34:1.

41. The various roles of state delegations are discussed in (ed.) Paul Tillet, *Inside Politics: The National Conventions 1960* (New Brunswick: Eagleton Institute, 1962).

42. Paul T. David, "The Primaries Are Deceptive," *The Washington Post,* July 21, 1968, B2:1; and Harris Survey reported in *The Washington Post,* July 8, 1968, A2:5.

43. David, *et. al., The Politics of National Party Conventions,* Chapter 12; Davis, *Presidential Primaries,* Chapter 4; Pomper, *Nominating the President,* pp. 105–133.

44. Louis Harris, "Why the Odds are Against a Governor's Becoming President," *Public Opinion Quarterly,* XXIII (Fall 1959), pp. 361–70.

45. Pomper, *Nominating the President,* pp. 48–54.

46. Summarized by Senator Edmund Muskie of Maine in a speech to the American Political Science Association, Washington, D.C., September 5, 1968; and *The New York Times.* December 1, 1968, 49:1, and March 2, 1969, 41:1.

47. Herring, *The Politics of Democracy,* p. 229.

48. Paul Tillet, "The National Conventions," *The Presidential Election and Transition,* in (ed.) Paul T. David. (Washington, D.C.: The Brookings Institution, 1961), pp. 54–55.

49. Truman, *The Governmental Process,* p. 285; and Pomper, *Nominating the President,* pp. 75-91.

50. Gerald Pomper, "If Elected, I Promise': American Party Platforms," *Midwest Journal of Political Science,* XI, No. 3 (August 1967), pp. 318–52. The relation between platform and party performance is explored further in his book, *Elections in America* (New York: Dodd, Mead, Inc., 1968) Chapters 7 and 8, will be discussed in Chapter VI also.

51. An excellent discussion is by Herbert McClosky, "Are Political Conventions Undemocratic?," *The New York Times,* August 4, 1968, pp. 10 ff.

52. *The New York Times,* October 27, 1968, 68:3.

53. *Ibid.,* 68:4.

54. This argument is drawn from and developed further by Dorothy James, *The Contemporary Presidency* (New York: Pegasus, 1969), Chapter 1.

55. Heard, *op. cit.,* pp. 375–77, provides the basis of the following argument.

56. Key, *Public Opinion and American Democracy,* pp. 547–51.

57. The typology discussed here and the concept of the "private partisan" were suggested by Gerald Pomper and a similar typology is part of his book *Elections in America* (New York: Dodd, Mead & Co., 1968), p. 69, with the term "private partisan" changed to "meddling partisan."

58. Campbell, *et. al., The American Voter,* pp. 550–51; and Berelson, *et. al., Voting,* pp. 305–23.

59. Maurice Carroll, "The Average Voter Is Not the Average American," *The New York Times,* November 3, 1968, 74:5.

60. Eugene Burdick, *The 480* (New York: McGraw-Hill Book Company, 1964); and *The Ninth Wave* (Boston: Houghton Mifflin Co., 1956).

61. A similar argument is found in Richard Rose and Harve Mossawir, "Voting and Elections: A Functional Analysis," *Political Studies,* XV, No. 2 (June 1967), pp. 173–201.

62. Key, *The Responsible Electorate,* pp. 16–18.

63. Pomper, *Elections in America,* pp. 228–43; and William R. Keech, *The Impact of Negro Voting* (Chicago: Rand McNally & Co., 1968), pp. 93–109.

Chapter VI. The Pervasiveness of Party in Government

1. Minnesota, a nonpartisan legislature, is organized by rival Liberal and Conservative causcuses, which substitute for the Democratic and Republican parties that operate in all other state legislatures, except Nebraska's.

2. Truman, *The Congressional Party,* pp. 193–236.

3. *Ibid.,* pp. 94–132.

4. Ralph Huitt, "Democratic Party Leadership in the Senate," *American Political Science Review,* LV, No. 2 (June 1961), pp. 335–37.

5. Jewell, *op. cit.,* pp. 93–103.

6. *Ibid.,* p. 104.

7. John Wahlke, *et. al., The Legislative System* (New York: John Wiley & Sons, Inc., 1962), pp. 363–64.

8. James D. Barber, *The Law Makers* (New Haven: Yale University Press, 1966), p. 61; and Sorauf, *Party and Representation,* pp. 144–46.

9. Schattschneider, *op. cit.,* p. 163–65.

10. *Ibid.,* pp. 165–68.

11. Jewell, *op. cit.,* pp. 119–27.

12. *Ibid.,* pp. 93–103.

13. Leon D. Epstein, "British M.P.s and Their Local Parties: The Suez Cases," *American Political Science Review,* LIV, No. 2 (June 1960), pp. 374–90; and "Cohesion of British Parlimentary Parties," *American Political Science Review,* L, No. 2 (June 1956), pp. 360–77.

14. John Wahlke, *et. al., The Legislative System,* Chapter 9.

15. Truman, *The Congressional Party,* pp. 143–44, 245–46. Also Randall B. Ripley, *Party Leaders in the House of Representatives* (Washington, D.C.: The Brookings Institution, 1967), especially Chapters 5 and 6, is relied upon in this section.

16. David R. Mayhew, *Party Loyalty Among Congressmen* (Cambridge, Mass.: Harvard University Press, 1966), pp. 146–47.

17. Jewell, *op. cit.,* p. 82.

18. *E.g.,* Truman, *The Congressional Party,* pp. 214–18; and Pertti Pesonen, "Close and Safe State Elections in Massachusetts," *Midwest Journal of Political Science,* VII, No. 2 (February 1963), pp. 66–67.

19. Ed Cray, "Jesse Unruh: 'Big Daddy' of California," *The Nation,* March 9, 1963; reprinted in (ed.) Russell W. Maddox, Jr., *Issues in State and Local Government* (Princeton, N.J.: D. Van Nostrand Co., Inc., 1965), pp. 151–59.

20. Truman, *The Congressional Party,* pp. 245–46.

21. Robert L. Peabody, "Party Leadership Change in the United States House of Representatives," *American Political Science Review,* LXI, No. 3 (September 1967), pp. 675–93.

22. Truman, *The Congressional Party,* pp. 133–44, 237–44.

23. *Ibid.,* pp. 297–99.

24. Jewell, *op. cit.,* pp. 112–27; Robert B. Highsaw, "The Southern Governor—Challenge to the Strong Executive Theme," *Public Administration Review,* XIX, No. 1 (1959), pp. 7–11; and Coleman B. Ransone, Jr., *The Office of Governor in the United States* (University, Ala.: University of Alabama Press, 1956), pp. 202–15.

25. Richard Neustadt, "Presidency and Legislation: Planning the President's Program," *American Political Science Review,* XLIV (December 1955), pp. 980–1021.

26. Truman, *The Congressional Party,* pp. 289–98.

27. *E.g.,* Wahlke, *et. al., The Legislative System,* pp. 272–80; and Dexter, "The Representative and His District."

28. Froman, *Congressmen and Their Constituencies,* pp. 92–95; Frank J. Sorauf, *Party and Representation,* pp. 32–41; and Duncan MacRae, Jr., "The Relation Between Roll Call Votes and Constituencies, in the Massachusetts House of Representatives," *American Political Science Review,* XLVI, No. 4 (December 1952), pp. 1046–55.

29. Key, *American State Politics,* pp. 152–53; and Donald Matthews, *U.S. Senators and Their World* (Chapel Hill, N.C.; University of North Carolina Press, 1960), pp. 35, 40–57.

30. Jewell, *op. cit.,* pp. 53–57, 75–76; and Sorauf, *Party and Representation,* pp. 147–54; and Samuel Huntington, "A Revised Theory of American Politics," *American Political Science Review,* XLIV, No. 3 (September 1950), pp. 669–77.

31. Mayhew, *op. cit.,* pp. 45–56, 146–68; the Republican Party in the House of Representatives does not use this "inclusive" strategy and has a greater constituency-party internal conflict.

32. Wahlke, *et. al., The Legislative System,* pp. 354–56.

33. Sorauf, *Party and Representation,* pp. 131–32, 140–43.

34. Stephen V. Monsuma, "Interpersonal Relations in the Legislative System," *Midwest Journal of Political Science,* X, No. 3 (August 1966), pp. 350–63; and Donald Matthews, *U.S. Senators and Their World.* This friendship effort is also found among party organization leaders; Thomas A. Flinn and Frederick M. Wirt, "Local Party Leaders: Groups of Like Minded Men," *Midwest Journal of Political Science,* IX, No. 1 (February 1965), pp. 77–98.

35. Ranney, "Parties in State Politics," p. 88; and Mayhew, *Party Loyalty Among Congressmen,* pp. 146–68.

36. Mayhew, *ibid.*

37. Truman, *The Congressional Party,* pp. 130, 205, 217, 225, 297.

38. Mayhew, *op. cit.,* pp. 27–28, 67–68, 98–100, 130–32, 148–49.

39. Important discussions of the issues involved are found in Wilder Crane, Jr., "Caveat on Roll-Call Studies of Party Voting," *Midwest Journal of Political Science,* IV, (1960), pp. 237–49; and Fred J. Greenstein and Elton F. Jackson, "A Second Look at the Validity of Roll-Call Analysis," *Midwest Journal of Political Science,* VIII, No. 2 (May 1963), pp. 156–66.

40. Truman, *The Congressional Party,* pp. 80–81, 86, 91–92, 182–85.

41. *Ibid.,* pp. 185–86, 218–19; having an incumbent President can force a shift in partisan position as it did for the Republicans under Eisenhower, Mayhew, pp. 24–6, 68–9.

42. Jewell, *op. cit.,* pp. 53–57, 75–76.

43. *Ibid.,* pp. 62–74.

44. The question of platform performance is fully discussed in Pomper, *Elections in America,* Chapter 8.

45. See notes 28 and 41 in this chapter; also Samuel C. Patterson, "Dimensions of Voting Behavior in a One-Party State Legislature," *Public Opinion Quarterly,* XXVI (Summer 1962), pp. 185–201.

46. *E.g.,* S. Sidney Ulmer, "The Political Party Variable in the Michigan Supreme Court," *Journal of Public Law,* II, No. 2 (1963), pp. 352–62, and Stuart S. Nagel, "Political Party Affiliation and Judges' Decisions," *American Political Science Review,* LV (1961), pp. 843–50.

47. *Ibid.*

48. Wilson, *The Amateur Democrat,* pp. 216–25. A partial exception to this thesis is found in Richard A. Watson, Ronald G. Downing, and Frederick C. Speigel, "Bar Politics, Judicial Selection and the Representation of Social Interests," *American Political Science Review,* LXI, No. 1 (March 1967), pp. 54–71.

49. This argument is developed more fully by Theodore J. Lowi, *At the Pleasure of the Mayor* (New York: The Free Press of Glencoe, 1964), pp. 215–31.

50. Theodore J. Lowi, "Party, Policy and Constitution in America," in (ed.) Chambers and Burnham, *The American Party Systems,* pp. 238–76, argues that channeling and moderating conflict are the dominant functions of American political parties.

Chapter VII. National Executive-centered Coalitions

1. Benjamin Baker and Stanley H. Friedelbaum, *Government in the United States* (Boston: Houghton Mifflin Company, 1966), p. 147.

2. *E.g.,* Truman, "Federalism and the Party System," pp. 115–36.

3. Cornelius P. Cotter and Bernard C. Hennessy, *Politics Without Power: the National Party Committee* (New York: Atherton Press, 1964), pp. 230–31.

4. Sorauf, *Political Parties in the American System,* pp. 40–41.

5. David J. Rothman, *Politics and Power: the United States Senate, 1869–1901* (Cambridge, Mass.: Harvard University Press, 1966), pp. 238–252.

6. Key, *American State Politics,* pp. 145–52.

7. Sorauf, *Political Parties in the American System,* pp. 40–41.

8. Ranney, *The Doctrine of Responsible Party Government,* pp. 15–16.

9. Bernard Berelson and Gary A. Steiner, *Human Behavior: An Inventory of Scientific Findings* (New York: Harcourt Brace & World, 1964), p. 384.

10. Truman, *The Governmental Process,* pp. 272–82.

11. Campbell, *et al., The American Voter,* pp. 227–34.

12. Clark and Wilson, "Incentive Systems: A Theory of Organizations," and Sorauf, "The Silent Revolution in Patronage."

13. Campbell, *et al., The American Voter,* pp. 148–49 and 164–67.

14. William H. Riker, *The Theory of Political Coalitions* (New Haven: Yale University Press, 1962), pp. 10–13.

15. The terminology of executive-centered coalitions comes from Robert A. Dahl, *Who Governs* (New Haven: Yale University Press, 1961), p. 200.

16. This line of argument parallels and develops the thesis stated by Arthur W. Macmahon, "Parties, Political-United States" in (ed.) Edwin R. A. Seligman, *Encyclopedia of the Social Sciences* (New York: The Macmillan Company, 1933), XI, pp. 596–601.

17. Campbell, *et al., The American Voter,* pp. 125–33.

18. See note 40 in Chapter IV.

19. Stokes, "Some Dynamic Elements of Contests for the Presidency."

20. This argument parallels the summary of the literature on leadership as situationally defined, found in John M. Pfiffner and Robert V. Presthus, *Public Administration,* 4th ed. (New York: The Ronald Press, 1960), pp. 92–97.

21. Campbell, *et al., The American Voter,* p. 82; and Stokes and Miller, "Party Government and the Saliency of Congress," p. 541.

22. Most discussions on this topic focus on the Presidency, *e.g.,* Malcolm Noos, *Politics, Presidents and Coattails* (Baltimore: Johns Hopkins Press, 1952); Warren E. Miller, "Presidential Coattails: A Study in Political Myth and Methodology." *Public Opinion Quarterly,* XIX (Winter 1955–56), pp. 26–39. Unpublished research by Donald Kaplan, "The Coattail Effect and American State Legislators" (New Brunswick, N.J., unpublished Henry Rutgers Essay, 1967), indicates the relevance of gubernatorial coattails.

23. Campbell, *et al., The American Voter,* pp. 45–53.

24. Stokes and Miller, "Party Government and the Saliency of Congress," and "Constituency Influence in Congress," and Stokes, "Parties and the Nationalization of Electoral Forces," in William N. Chambers and Walter D. Burnham (eds.), *The American Party Systems,* pp. 182–202.

25. Samuel C. Patterson, "Dimensions of Voting Behavior in a One-Party State Legislature;" and *Congressmen and Their Constituencies,* pp. 116–17.

26. Hyman, *op cit.,* and Berelson, *et al., Voting,* suggests the mechanisms by which this is accomplished.

27. Seymour M. Lipset, *Political Man* (Garden City, N.Y.: Doubleday, Inc., 1960), pp. 294–98.

28. Pomper, *Elections in America,* Chapters 7 and 8.

29. Campbell, *et al., The American Voter,* pp. 136–42.

30. Samuel J. Eldersveld, *Political Parties* (Chicago: Rand McNally & Co., 1964), pp. 118–34, and Wahlke, *et al., The Legislative System,* pp. 77–94.

31. Wahlke, *et al., The Legislative System,* pp. 351–69, and Monsma, "Interpersonal Relations in the Legislative System," pp. 350–63, and Flinn and Wirt, "Local Party Leaders: Groups of Like Minded Men."

32. Herbert McCloskey, *et al.*, "Issue Conflict and Consensus in American Party Leaders and Followers," *American Political Science Review,* LIV (1960), pp. 406–27; and Flinn and Wirt, *op. cit.*

33. Among the most important of these are: Truman, *The Congressional Party;* Julius Turner, *Party and Constituency: Pressures on Congress* (Baltimore: The Johns Hopkins Press, 1951); Malcolm E. Jewell, *The State Legislature;* and Froman, *op. cit.*

34. Key, *American State Politics,* Chapter 8; Frank J. Sorauf, *Party and Representation,* pp. 32–41; and Froman, *op. cit.*, pp. 14, 91–92, 118.

35. Sorauf, *Party and Representation,* pp. 65–75.

36. Key, *American State Politics,* pp. 152–65.

37. Stokes and Miller, "Constituency Influence in Congress," pp. 48–52; Lewis A. Dexter, "The Representative and His District"; and Froman, *op. cit.*, p. 14.

38. Froman, *op. cit.*, p. 5, and Mayhew, *Party Loyalty Among Congressmen,* pp. 146–68, especially for Democrats in Congress.

39. Cf. note 33 in this chapter.

40. Mayew, *op. cit.*, shows reciprocity on constituency interests reinforcing and rewarding party loyalty; this modifies somewhat the emphasis of Froman, *op. cit.*, pp. 6–10, but his evidence does not seem to require a conflict interpretation.

41. Nagel, "Political Party Affiliation and Judges' Decisions," and Ulmer, "The Political Party Variable in the Michigan Supreme Court."

42. Dahl, *op. cit.*, pp. 186–88. It is important to note that the description of parties as executive centered is not intended to be a prescriptive statement.

43. Roger Davidson, David M. Kovenock, and Michael K. O'Leary, *Congress in Crises: Politics and Congressional Reform* (Belmont, Cal.; Wadsworth Publishing Co., Inc., 1966), pp. 59–63. In other words, prescriptive attitudes favoring executive priority help create the descriptive fact of executive priority.

44. Neustadt, "Presidency and Legislation: Planning the President's Program," Ransome, *The Office of Governor in the United States;* and Jewell, *op. cit.*, pp. 107–19. Further emphasizing executive visibility, G. Cleveland Wilhoit and Kenneth S. Sherrill, "Wire Service Visibility of U.S. Senators," *Journalism Quarterly,* XLV, No. 1 (Spring 1968), pp. 42–8, find that four of the five most frequently mentioned senators are Presidential candidates or elected leaders of the legislative party.

45. Truman, *The Congressional Party,* pp. 280–89.

46. Cotter and Hennessy, *op. cit.*, pp. 231–33; Macmahon, "Parties, Political-United States," p. 597.

47. Truman, *The Congressional Party,* pp. 308–16.

48. Stokes and Miller, "Party Government and the Saliency of Congress," p. 536.

49. David, Goldman, and Bain, *The Politics of National Party Conventions,* pp. 75–87, 106–10.

50. Paul T. David, "The Changing Political Parties", pp. 56–57; and Stokes, "Parties and the Nationalization of Electoral Forces."

51. Pomper, *Nominating The President,* pp. 66–91.

52. Macmahon, "Parties, Political-United States," p. 596.

53. Campbell, *et. al.*, *The American Voter,* p. 184. They were reinforced by the recessions of the Eisenhower Administration, especially in 1958.

54. Donald R. Matthews and James W. Prothro, *Negroes and the New Southern Politics* (New York: Harcourt, Brace & World, 1966), pp. 378–84, and Campbell, *et al., The American Voter,* pp. 185–86, 556–57.

55. Key, *American State Politics,* pp. 40–41.

56. *Ibid.,* Chapter 2.

57. *Ibid.,* p. 33.

Chapter VIII. Conclusion

1. It is important to note that the trend away from regionalism in the United States may be overrated, Noval G. Glenn and J. L. Simmons, "Are Regional Cultural Differences Diminishing?", *Public Opinion Quarterly,* XXXI, No. 2 (Summer 1967), pp. 176–93, and Frank Munger and James Blackhurst, "Factionalism in the National Conventions, 1940–64. An Analysis of Ideological Consistency in State Delegation Voting," *Journal of Politics,* XXVII (1965), pp. 375–94.

2. This and related arguments are developed more fully by David, "The Changing Political Parties," pp. 53–64.

3. For 1964 see Thomas W. Benham, "Polling For a Presidential Candidate: Some Observations on the 1964 Campaign," *Public Opinion Quarterly,* XXIX, No. 2 (Summer 1965), p. 192, and for 1968 see *The New York Times,* Oct. 27, 1968, 68:3.

4. Robert C. Wood, *Suburbia: Its People and Their Politics* (Boston: Houghton Mifflin Co., 1959), pp. 153–61.

5. Dennis, "Support for the Party System by the Mass Public."

index